The Old Northwest,

A Chronicle Of The Ohio Valley And Beyond

Frederic Austin Ogg

The Old Northwest

Frederic Austin Ogg

© 1st World Library – Literary Society, 2004
PO Box 2211
Fairfield, IA 52556
www.1stworldlibrary.org
First Edition

LCCN: 2004117754

Softcover ISBN: 1-4218-0125-6
Hardcover ISBN: 1-4218-0025-X
eBook ISBN: 1-4218-0225-2

Purchase *"The Old Northwest"*
as a traditional bound book at:
www.1stWorldLibrary.org/purchase.asp?ISBN=1-4218-0125-6

1st World Library Literary Society is a nonprofit organization dedicated to promoting literacy by:

- Creating a free internet library accessible from any computer worldwide.
- Hosting writing competitions and offering book publishing scholarships.

Readers interested in supporting literacy through sponsorship, donations or membership please contact:
literacy@1stworldlibrary.org
Check us out at: www.1stworldlibrary.ORG
and start downloading free ebooks today.

The Old Northwest
*contributed by Tim, Ed & Rodney
in support of
1st World Library Literary Society*

CONTENTS

I. PONTIAC'S CONSPIRACY........................ 7

II. A LAIR OF WILD BEASTS........................21

III. THE REVOLUTION BEGINS..................... 36

IV. THE CONQUEST COMPLETED...................47

V. WAYNE, THE SCOURGE OF THE INDIANS.........61

VI. THE GREAT MIGRATION....................... 76

VII. PIONEER DAYS AND WAYS.................... 86

VIII. TECUMSEH................................. 101

IX. THE WAR OF 1812 AND THE NEW WEST........ 116

X. SECTIONAL CROSS CURRENTS.................. 132

XI. THE UPPER MISSISSIPPI VALLEY...............144

BIBLIOGRAPHICAL NOTE....................... 159

Chapter I.

Pontiac's Conspiracy

The fall of Montreal, on September 8, 1760, while the plains about the city were still dotted with the white tents of the victorious English and colonial troops, was indeed an event of the deepest consequence to America and to the world. By the articles of capitulation which were signed by the Marquis de Vaudreuil, Governor of New France, Canada and all its dependencies westward to the Mississippi passed to the British Crown. Virtually ended was the long struggle for the dominion of the New World. Open now for English occupation and settlement was that vast country lying south of the Great Lakes between the Ohio and the Mississippi - which we know as the Old Northwest - today the seat of five great commonwealths of the United States.

With an ingenuity born of necessity, the French pathfinders and colonizers of the Old Northwest had chosen for their settlements sites which would serve at once the purposes of the priest, the trader, and the soldier; and with scarcely an exception these sites are as important today as when they were first selected. Four regions, chiefly, were still occupied by the French at the time of the capitulation of Montreal. The most important, as well as the most distant, of these regions was on the east bank of the Mississippi, opposite and below the present city of St. Louis, where a cluster of missions, forts, and trading-posts held the center of the tenuous line extending from Canada to Louisiana. A second was the Illinois country, centering about the citadel of St. Louis which La Salle had erected in 1682 on the summit of "Starved Rock," near the modern town of Ottawa in Illinois. A third was the valley of the Wabash, where in the early years of the eighteenth century Vincennes had become the seat of a colony commanding both the Wabash and the lower Ohio. And the fourth was the western end of Lake Erie, where Detroit, founded by the doughty Cadillac in 1701, had assumed such strength that for fifty years it had discouraged the ambitions of the English to make the Northwest theirs.

Sir Jeffrey Amherst, to whom Vaudreuil surrendered in 1760, forthwith dispatched to the western country a military force to take possession of the posts still remaining in the hands of the French. The mission was entrusted to a stalwart New Hampshire Scotch-Irishman, Major Robert Rogers, who as leader of a band of intrepid "rangers" had made himself the hero of the northern frontier. Two hundred men were chosen for the undertaking, and on the 13th of September the party, in fifteen whaleboats, started up the St. Lawrence for Detroit.

At the mouth of the Cuyahoga River, near the site of the present city of Cleveland, the travelers were halted by a band of Indian chiefs and warriors who, in the name of their great ruler Pontiac, demanded to know the object of their journeying. Parleys followed, in which Pontiac himself took part, and it was explained that the French had surrendered Canada to the English and that the English merely proposed to assume control of the western posts, with a view to friendly relations between the red men and the white men. The rivers, it was promised, would flow with rum, and presents from the great King would be forthcoming in endless profusion. The explanation seemed to satisfy the savages, and, after smoking the calumet with due ceremony, the chieftain and his followers withdrew.

Late in November, Rogers and his men in their whaleboats appeared before the little palisaded town of Detroit. They found the French commander, Beletre, in surly humor and seeking to stir up the neighboring Wyandots and Potawatomi against them. But the attempt failed, and there was nothing for Beletre to do but yield. The French soldiery marched out of the fort, laid down their arms, and were sent off as prisoners down the river. The fleur-de-lis, which for more than half a century had floated over the village, was hauled down, and, to the accompaniment of cheers, the British ensign was run up. The red men looked on with amazement at this display of English authority and marveled how the conquerors forbore to slay their vanquished enemies on the spot.

Detroit in 1760 was a picturesque, lively, and rapidly growing frontier town. The central portions of the settlement, lying within the bounds of the present city, contained ninety or a hundred small houses, chiefly of wood and roofed with bark or thatch. A well-built range of barracks afforded quarters for the soldiery, and there were two public buildings - a council house and a little church. The whole was surrounded by a square palisade twenty-five feet high, with a wooden bastion at each corner and a blockhouse over each gateway. A broad passageway, the chemin du ronde, lay next to the palisade, and on little narrow streets at the center the houses were grouped closely together.

Above and below the fort the banks of the river were lined on both sides, for a distance of eight or nine miles, with little rectangular farms, so laid out as to give each a water-landing. On each farm was a cottage, with a garden and orchard, surrounded by a fence of rounded pickets; and the countryside rang with the shouts and laughter of a prosperous and happy peasantry. Within the limits of the settlement were villages of Ottawas, Potawatomi, and Wyandots, with whose inhabitants the French lived on free and easy terms. "The joyous sparkling of the bright blue water," writes Parkman; "the green luxuriance of the woods; the white dwellings, looking out from the foliage; and in the distance the Indian wigwams curling their smoke against the sky - all were mingled in one broad scene of wild and rural beauty."

At the coming of the English the French residents were given an opportunity to withdraw. Few, however, did so, and from the gossipy correspondence of the pleasure-loving Colonel Campbell, who for some months was left in command of the fort, it appears that the life of the place lost none of its gayety by the change of masters. Sunday card parties at the quarters of the commandant were festive affairs; and at a ball held in celebration of the King's birthday the ladies presented an appearance so splendid as to call forth from the impressionable officer the most extravagant praises. A visit in the summer of 1761 from Sir William Johnson, general supervisor of Indian affairs on the frontier, became the greatest social event in the history of the settlement, if not of the entire West. Colonel Campbell gave a ball at which the guests danced nine hours. Sir William reciprocated with one at which they danced eleven hours. A round of dinners and calls gave opportunity for much display of frontier magnificence, as well as for the consumption of astonishing quantities of wines and cordials. Hundreds of Indians were interested spectators, and the gifts with which they were generously showered were received with evidences of deep satisfaction.

No amount of fiddling and dancing, however, could quite drown apprehension concerning the safety of the post and the security of the English hold upon the great region over which this fort and its distant neighbors stood sentinel. Thousands of square miles of territory were committed to the keeping of not more than six hundred soldiers. From the French there was little danger. But from the Indians anything might be expected. Apart from the Iroquois, the red men had been bound to the French by many ties of friendship and common interest, and in the late war they had scalped and slaughtered and burned unhesitatingly at the French command. Hardly, indeed, had the transfer of territorial sovereignty been made before murmurs of discontent began to be heard.

Notwithstanding outward expressions of assent to the new order of things, a deep-rooted dislike on the part of the Indians for the English grew after 1760 with great rapidity. They sorely missed the gifts and supplies lavishly provided by the French, and they warmly resented the rapacity and arrogance of the British traders. The open contempt of the soldiery at the posts galled the Indians, and the confiscation of their lands drove them to desperation. In their hearts hope never died that the French would regain their lost dominion; and again and again rumors were set afloat that this was about to happen. The belief in such a reconquest was adroitly encouraged, too, by the surviving French settlers and traders. In 1761 the tension among the Indians was increased by the appearance of a "prophet" among the Delawares, calling on all his race to purge itself of foreign influences and to unite to drive the white man from the land.

Protests against English encroachments were frequent and, though respectful, none the less emphatic. At a conference in Philadelphia in 1761, an Iroquois sachem declared, "We, your Brethren, of the several Nations, are penned up like Hoggs. There are Forts all around us, and therefore we are apprehensive that Death is coming upon us." "We are now left in Peace," ran a petition of some Christian Oneidas addressed to Sir William Johnson, "and have nothing to do but to plant our Corn, Hunt the wild Beasts, smoke our Pipes, and mind Religion. But as these Forts, which are built among us, disturb our Peace, and are a great hurt to Religion, because some of our Warriors are foolish, and some of our Brother Soldiers don't fear God, we therefore desire that these Forts may be pull'd down, and kick'd out of the way."

The leadership of the great revolt that was impending fell naturally upon Pontiac, who, since the coming of the English, had established himself with his squaws and children on a wooded island in Lake St. Clair, barely out of view of the fortifications of Detroit. In all Indian annals no name is more illustrious than Pontiac's; no figure more forcefully displays the good and bad qualities of his race. Principal chief of the Ottawa tribe, he was also by 1763 the head of a powerful confederation of Ottawas, Ojibwas, and Potawatomi, and a leader known and respected among

Algonquin peoples from the sources of the Ohio to the Mississippi. While capable of acts of magnanimity, he had an ambition of Napoleonic proportions, and to attain his ends he was prepared to use any means. More clearly than most of his forest contemporaries, he perceived that in the life of the Indian people a crisis had come. He saw that, unless the tide of English invasion was rolled back at once, all would be lost. The colonial farmers would push in after the soldiers; the forests would be cut away; the hunting-grounds would be destroyed; the native population would be driven away or enslaved. In the silence of his wigwam he thought out a plan of action, and by the closing weeks of 1762 he was ready. Never was plot more shrewdly devised and more artfully carried out.

During the winter of 1762-63 his messengers passed stealthily from nation to nation throughout the whole western country, bearing the pictured wampum belts and the reddened tomahawks which symbolized war; and in April, 1763, the Lake tribes were summoned to a great council on the banks of the Ecorces, below Detroit, where Pontiac in person proclaimed the will of the Master of Life as revealed to the Delaware prophet, and then announced the details of his plan. Everywhere the appeal met with approval; and not only the scores of Algonquin peoples, but also the Seneca branch of the Iroquois confederacy and a number of tribes on the lower Mississippi, pledged themselves with all solemnity to fulfill their prophet's injunction "to drive the dogs which wear red clothing into the sea." While keen-eyed warriors sought to keep up appearances by lounging about the forts and begging in their customary manner for tobacco, whiskey, and gun-powder, every wigwam and forest hamlet from Niagara to the Mississippi was astir. Dusky maidens chanted the tribal war-songs, and in the blaze of a hundred camp-fires chiefs and warriors performed the savage pantomime of battle.

A simultaneous attack, timed by a change of the moon, was to be made on the English forts and settlements throughout all the western country. Every tribe was to fall upon the settlement nearest at hand, and afterwards all were to combine - with French aid, it was confidently believed - in an assault on the seats of English power farther east. The honor of destroying the most important of the English strongholds, Detroit, was reserved for Pontiac himself.

The date fixed for the rising was the 7th of May. Six days in advance Pontiac with forty of his warriors appeared at the fort, protested undying friendship for the Great Father across the water, and insisted on performing the calumet dance before the new commandant, Major Gladwyn. This aroused no suspicion. But four days later a French settler reported that his wife, when visiting the Ottawa village to buy venison, had observed the men busily filing off the ends of their gunbarrels; and the blacksmith at the post recalled the fact that the Indians had lately sought to borrow files and saws without being able to give a plausible explanation of the use they intended to make of the implements.

The English traveler Jonathan Carver, who visited the post five years afterwards, relates that an Ottawa girl with whom Major Gladwyn had formed an attachment betrayed the plot. Though this story is of doubtful authenticity, there is no doubt that, in one way or another, the commandant was amply warned that treachery was in the air. The sounds of revelry from the Indian camps, the furtive glances of the redskins lounging about the settlement, the very tension of the atmosphere, would have been enough to put an experienced Indian fighter on his guard.

Accordingly when, on the fated morning, Pontiac and sixty redskins, carrying under long blankets their shortened muskets, appeared before the fort and asked admission, they were taken aback to find the whole garrison under arms. On their way from the gate to the council house they were obliged to march literally between rows of glittering steel. Well might even Pontiac falter. With uneasy glances, the party crowded into the council room, where Gladwyn and his officers sat waiting. "Why," asked the chieftain stolidly, "do I see so many of my father's young men standing in the street with their guns?" "To keep them in training," was the laconic reply.

The scene that was planned was then carried out, except in one vital particular. When, in the course of his speech professing strong attachment to the English, the chieftain came to the point where he was to give the signal for slaughter by holding forth the wampum belt of peace inverted, he presented the emblem - to the accompaniment of a significant clash of arms and roll of drums from the mustered garrison outside - in the normal manner; and after a solemn warning from the commandant that vengeance would follow any act of aggression, the council broke up. To the forest leader's equivocal announcement that he would bring all of his wives and children in a few days to shake hands with their English fathers, Gladwyn deigned no reply.

Balked in his plans, the chief retired, but only to meditate fresh treachery; and when, a few days later, with a multitude of followers, he sought admission to the fort to assure "his fathers" that "evil birds had sung lies in their ears," and was refused, he called all his forces to arms, threw off his disguises, and began hostilities. For six months the settlement was besieged with a persistence rarely displayed in Indian warfare. At first the French inhabitants encouraged the besiegers, but, after it became known that a final peace between England and France had been concluded, they withheld further aid. Throughout the whole period, the English obtained supplies with no great difficulty from the neighboring farms. There was little actual fighting, and the loss of life was insignificant.

By order of General Amherst, the French commander still in charge of Fort Chartres sent a messenger to inform the redskins definitely that no assistance from France would be forthcoming. "Forget then, my dear children," - so ran the admonition - "all evil talks. Leave off from spilling the blood of your brethren, the English. Our hearts are now but one; you cannot, at present, strike the one without having the other for an enemy also." The effect was, as intended, to break the spirit of the besiegers; and in October Pontiac humbly sued for peace.

Meanwhile a reign of terror spread over the entire frontier. Settlements from Forts Le Boeuf and Venango, south of Lake Erie, to Green Bay, west of Lake Michigan, were attacked, and ruses similar to that attempted at Detroit were generally successful. A few Indians in friendly guise would approach a fort. After these were admitted, others would appear, as if quite by chance. Finally, when numbers were sufficient, the conspirators would draw their concealed weapons, strike down the garrison, and begin a general massacre of the helpless populace. Scores of pioneer families, scattered through the wilderness, were murdered and scalped; traders were waylaid in the forest solitudes; border towns were burned and plantations were devastated. In the Ohio Valley everything was lost except Fort Pitt, formerly Fort Duquesne; in the Northwest, everything was taken except Detroit.

Fort Pitt was repeatedly endangered, and the most important engagement of the war was fought in its defense. The relief of the post was entrusted in midsummer to a force of five hundred regulars lately transferred from the West Indies to Pennsylvania and placed under the command of Colonel Henry Bouquet. The expedition advanced with all possible caution, but early in August, 1763, when it was yet twenty-five miles from its destination, it was set upon by a formidable Indian band at Bushy Run and threatened with a fate not un-like that suffered by Braddock's little army in the same region nine years earlier. Finding the woods full of redskins and all retreat cut off, the troops, drawn up in a circle around their horses and supplies, fired with such effect as they could upon the shadowy forms in the forest. No water was obtainable, and in a few hours thirst began to make the soldiery unmanageable. Realizing that the situation was desperate, Bouquet resorted to a ruse by ordering his men to fall back as if in retreat. The trick succeeded, and with yells of victory the Indians rushed from cover to seize the coveted provisions - only to be met by a deadly fire and put to utter rout. The news of the battle of Bushy Run spread rapidly through the frontier regions and proved very effective in discouraging further hostilities.

It was Bouquet's intention to press forward at once

from Fort Pitt into the disturbed Ohio country. His losses, however, compelled the postponement of this part of the undertaking until the following year. Before he started off again he built at Fort Pitt a blockhouse which still stands, and which has been preserved for posterity by becoming, in 1894, the property of the Pittsburgh chapter of the Daughters of the American Revolution. In October, 1764, he set out for the Muskingum valley with a force of fifteen hundred regulars, Pennsylvania and Virginia volunteers, and friendly Indians. By this time the great conspiracy was in collapse, and it was a matter of no great difficulty for Bouquet to enter into friendly relations with the successive tribes, to obtain treaties with them, and to procure the release of such English captives as were still in their hands. By the close of November, 1764, the work was complete, and Bouquet was back at Fort Pitt. Pennsylvania and Virginia honored him with votes of thanks; the King formally expressed his gratitude and tendered him the military governorship of the newly acquired territory of Florida.

The general pacification of the Northwest was accomplished by treaties with the natives in great councils held at Niagara, Presqu'isle (Erie), and Detroit. Pontiac had fled to the Maumee country to the west of Lake Erie, whence he still hurled his ineffectual threats at the "dogs in red." His power, however, was broken. The most he could do was to gather four hundred warriors on the Maumee and Illinois and present himself at Fort Chartres with a demand for weapons and ammunition with which to keep up the war. The French commander, who was now daily awaiting orders to turn the fortress over to the English, refused; and a deputation dispatched to New Orleans in quest of the desired equipment received no reply save that New Orleans itself, with all the country west of the river, had been ceded to Spain. The futility of further resistance on the part of Pontiac was apparent. In 1765 the disappointed chieftain gave pledges of friendship; and in the following year he and other leaders made a formal submission to Sir William Johnson at Oswego, and Pontiac renounced forever the bold design to make himself at a stroke lord of the West and deliverer of his country from English domination.

For three years the movements of this disappointed Indian leader are uncertain. Most of the time, apparently, he dwelt in the Maumee country, leading the existence of an ordinary warrior. Then, in the spring of 1769, he appeared at the settlements on the middle Mississippi. At the newly founded French town of St. Louis, on the Spanish side of the river, he visited an old friend, the commandant Saint Ange de Bellerive. Thence he crossed to Cahokia, where Indian and creole alike welcomed him and made him the central figure in a series of boisterous festivities.

An English trader in the village, observing jealously the honors that were paid the visitor, resolved that an old score should forthwith be evened up. A Kaskaskian redskin was bribed, with a barrel of liquor and with promises of further reward, to put the fallen leader out of the way; and the bargain was hardly sealed before the deed was done. Stealing upon his victim as he walked in the neighboring forest, the assassin buried a tomahawk in his brain, and "thus basely," in the words of Parkman, "perished the champion of a ruined race." Claimed by Saint-Ange, the body was borne across the river and buried with military honors near the new Fort St. Louis. The site of Pontiac's grave was soon forgotten, and today the people of a great city trample over and about it without heed.

Chapter II.

A Lair Of Wild Beasts

Benjamin Franklin, who was in London in 1760 as agent of the Pennsylvania Assembly, gave the British ministers some wholesome advice on the terms of the peace that should be made with France. The St. Lawrence and the Great Lakes regions, he said, must be retained by England at all costs. Moreover, the Mississippi Valley must be taken, in order to provide for the growing populations of the seaboard colonies suitable lands in the interior, and so keep them engaged in agriculture. Otherwise these populations would turn to manufacturing, and the industries of the mother country would suffer.

The treaty of peace, three years later, brought the settlement which Franklin suggested. The vast American back country, with its inviting rivers and lakes, its shaded hills, and its sunny prairies, became English territory. The English people had, however, only the vaguest notion of the extent, appearance, and resources of their new possession. Even the officials who drew the treaty were as ignorant of the country as of middle Africa. Prior to the outbreak of the war no widely known English writer had tried to describe it; and the absorbing French books of Lahontan, Hennepin, and Charlevoix had reached but a small circle. The prolonged conflict in America naturally stimulated interest in the new country. The place-names of the upper Ohio became household words, and enterprising publishers put out not only translations of the French writers but compilations by Englishmen designed, in true journalistic fashion, to meet the demands of the hour for information.

These publications displayed amazing misconceptions of the lands described. They neither estimated aright the number and strength of the French settlements nor dispelled the idea that the western country was of little value. Even the most brilliant Englishman of the day, Dr. Samuel Johnson, an ardent defender of the treaty of 1763, wrote that the large tracts of America added by the war to the British dominions were "only the barren parts of the continent, the refuse of the earlier adventurers, which the French, who came last, had taken only as better than nothing." As late indeed as 1789, William Knox, long Under-Secretary for the Colonies, declared that Americans could not settle the western territory "for ages," and that the region must be given up to barbarism like the plains of Asia, with a population as unstable as the Scythians and Tartars. But the shortsightedness of these distant critics can be forgiven when one recalls that Franklin himself, while conjuring up a splendid vision of the western valleys teeming with a thriving population, supposed that the dream would not be realized for "some centuries." None of these observers dreamt that the territories transferred in 1763 would have within seventy-five years a population almost equal to that of Great Britain.

The ink with which the Treaty of Paris was signed was hardly dry before the King and his ministers were confronted with the task of providing government for the new possessions and of solving problems of land tenure and trade. Still more imperative were measures to conciliate the Indians; for already Pontiac's rebellion had been in progress four months, and the entire back country was aflame. It must be confessed that a continental wilderness swarming with murderous savages was an inheritance whose aspect was by no means altogether pleasing to the English mind.

The easiest solution of the difficulty was to let things take their course. Let seaboard populations spread at will over the new lands; let them carry on trade in their own way, and make whatever arrangements with the native tribes they desire. Colonies such as Virginia and New York, which had extensive western claims, would have been glad to see this plan adopted. Strong objections, however, were raised. Colonies which had no western claims feared the effects of the advantages which their more fortunate neighbors would enjoy. Men who had invested heavily in lands lying west of the mountains felt that their returns would be diminished and delayed if the back country were thrown open to settlers. Some people thought that the Indians had a moral right to protection against wholesale white invasion of their hunting-grounds, and many considered it expedient, at all events, to offer such protection.

After all, however, it was the King and his ministers who had it in their power to settle the question; and from their point of view it was desirable to keep the western territories as much as possible apart from the older colonies, and to regulate, with farsighted policy, their settlement and trade. Eventually, it was believed, the territories would be cut into new colonies; and experience with the seaboard dependencies was already such as to suggest the desirability of having the future settlements more completely under government control from the beginning.

After due consideration, King George and his ministers made known their policy on October 7, 1763, in a comprehensive proclamation. The first subject dealt with was government. Four new provinces - "Quebec, East Florida, West Florida, and Grenada"* - were set up in the ceded territories, and their populations were guaranteed all the rights and privileges enjoyed by the inhabitants of the older colonies. The Mississippi Valley, however, was included in no one of these provinces; and, curiously, there was no provision whatever for the government of the French settlements lying within it. The number and size of these settlements were underestimated, and apparently it was supposed that all the habitants and soldiers would avail themselves of their privilege of withdrawing from the ceded territories.

* The Proclamation of 1763 drew the boundaries of "four distinct and separate governments." Grenada was to include the island of that name, together with the Grenadines. Dominico, St. Vincent, and Tobago. The Floridas lay south of the bounds of Georgia and east of the Mississippi River. The Apalachicola River was to be the dividing line between East and West Florida. Quebec included the modern province of that name and that part of Ontario lying north of a line drawn from Lake Nipissing to the point where the forty-fifth parallel intersects the St. Lawrence River.

The disposition made of the great rectangular area bounded by the Alleghanies, the Mississippi, the

Lakes, and the Gulf, was fairly startling. With fine disregard of the chartered claims of the seaboard colonies and of the rights of pioneers already settled on frontier farms, the whole was erected into an Indian reserve. No "loving subject" might purchase land or settle in the territory without special license; present residents should "forthwith remove themselves"; trade should be carried on only by permit and under close surveillance; officers were to be stationed among the tribes to preserve friendly relations and to apprehend fugitives from colonial justice.

The objects of this drastic scheme were never clearly stated. Franklin believed that the main purpose was to conciliate the Indians. Washington agreed with him. Later historians have generally thought that what the English Government had chiefly in mind was to limit the bounds of the seaboard colonies, with a view to preserving imperial control over colonial affairs. Very likely both of these motives weighed heavily in the decision. At all events, Lord Hillsborough, who presided over the meetings of the Lords of Trade when the proclamation was discussed, subsequently wrote that the "capital object" of the Government's policy was to confine the colonies so that they should be kept in easy reach of British trade and of the authority necessary to keep them in due subordination to the mother country, and he added that the extension of the fur trade depended "entirely upon the Indians being undisturbed in the possession of their hunting-grounds."*

* But as Lord Hillsborough had just taken office and adopted bodily a policy formulated by his predecessor, he is none too good an authority. See Alvord's "Mississippi Valley in British Politics," vol. I, pp. 203-4.

It does not follow that the King and his advisers intended that the territory should be kept forever intact as a forest preserve. They seem to have contemplated that, from time to time, cessions would be secured from the Indians and tracts would be opened for settlement. But every move was to be made in accordance with plans formulated or authorized in England. The restrictive policy won by no means universal assent in the mother country. The Whigs generally opposed it, and Burke thundered against it as "an attempt to keep as a lair of wild beasts that earth which God, by an express charter, has given to the children of men."

In America there was a disposition to take the proclamation lightly as being a mere sop to the Indians. But wherever it was regarded seriously, it was hotly resented. After passing through an arduous war, the colonists were ready to enter upon a new expansive era. The western territories were theirs by charter, by settlement, and by conquest. The Indian population, they believed, belonged to the unprogressive and unproductive peoples of the earth. Every acre of fertile soil in America called to the thrifty agriculturist; every westward flowing river invited to trade and settlement as well, therefore, seek to keep back the ocean with a broom as to stop by mere decree the tide of home-seekers. Some of the colonies made honest attempts to compel the removal of settlers from the reserved lands beyond their borders, and Pennsylvania went so far as to decree the death penalty for all who should refuse to remove. But the law was never enforced.

The news of the cession of the eastern bank of the Mississippi to the English brought consternation to the two or three thousand French people living in the settlements of the Kaskaskia, Illinois, and Wabash regions. The transfer of the western bank to Spain did not become known promptly, and for months the habitants supposed that by taking up their abode on the opposite side of the stream they would continue under their own flag. Many of them crossed the Mississippi to find new abodes even after it was announced that the land had passed to Spain.

From first to last these settlements on the Mississippi, the Wabash, and the Illinois had remained, in French hands, mere sprawling villages. The largest of them, Kaskaskia, may have contained in its most flourishing days two thousand people, many of them voyageurs, coureurs-de-bois, converted Indians, and transients of one sort or another. In 1765 there were not above seventy permanent families. Few of the towns, indeed, attained a population of more than two or three hundred. All French colonial enterprise had been based on the assumption that settlers would be few. The trader preferred it so, because settlements meant restrictions upon his traffic. The Jesuit was of the same mind, because such settlements broke up his mission field. The Government at Paris forbade the emigration of the one class of people that cared to emigrate, the Huguenots.

Though some of the settlements had picturesque sites and others drew distinction from their fortifications, in general they presented a drab appearance. There were usually two or three long, narrow streets, with no paving, and often knee-deep with mud. The houses were built on either side, at intervals sufficient to give space for yards and garden plots, each homestead being enclosed with a crude picket fence. Wood and thatch were the commonest building materials, although stone was sometimes used; and the houses were regularly one story high, with large vine-covered verandas. Land was abundant and cheap. Every enterprising settler had a plot for himself, and as a rule one large field, or more, was held for use in common. In these, the operations of ploughing, sowing, and reaping were carefully regulated by public ordinance. Occasionally a village drew some distinction from the proximity of a large, well-managed estate, such as that of the opulent M. Beauvais of Kaskaskia, in whose mill and brewery more than eighty slaves were employed.

Agriculture was carried on somewhat extensively, and it is recorded that, in the year 1746 alone, when there was a shortage of foodstuffs at New Orleans, the Illinois settlers were able to send thither "upward of eight hundred thousand weight of flour." Hunting and trading, however, continued to be the principal occupations; and the sugar, indigo, cotton, and other luxuries which the people were able to import directly from Europe were paid for mainly with consignments of furs, hides, tallow, and beeswax. Money was practically unknown in the settlements, so that domestic trade likewise took the form of simple barter. Periods of industry and prosperity alternated with periods of depression, and the easy-going habitants - "farmers, hunters, traders by turn, with a strong admixture of unprogressive Indian blood" - tended always to relapse into utter indolence.

Some of these French towns, however, were seats of culture; and none was wholly barren of diversions. Kaskaskia had a Jesuit college and likewise a monastery. Cahokia had a school for Indian youth. Fort Chartres, we are gravely told, was "the center of life and fashion in the West." If everyday existence was humdrum, the villagers had always the opportunity for voluble conversation "each from his own balcony"; and there were scores of Church festivals, not to mention birthdays, visits of travelers or neighbors, and homecomings of hunters and traders, which invited to festivity. Balls and dances and other merrymakings at which the whole village assembled supplied the wants of a people proverbially fond of amusement. Indeed, French civilization in the Mississippi and Illinois country was by no means without charm.

Kaskaskia, in the wonderfully fertile "American Bottom," maintained its existence, in spite of the cession to the English, as did also Vincennes farther east on the Wabash. Fort Chartres, a stout fortification whose walls were more than two feet thick, remained the seat of the principal garrison, and some traces of French occupancy survived on the Illinois. Cahokia was deserted, save for the splendid mission-farm of St. Sulpice, with its thirty slaves, its herd of cattle, and its mill, which the fathers before returning to France sold to a thrifty Frenchman not averse to becoming an English subject. A few posts were abandoned altogether. Some of the departing inhabitants went back to France; some followed the French commandant, Neyon de Villiers, down the river to New Orleans; many gathered up their possessions, even to the frames and clapboards of their houses, and took refuge in the new towns which sprang up on the western bank. One of these new settlements was Ste. Genevieve, strategically located near the lead mines from which the entire region had long drawn its supplies of shot. Another, which was destined to greater importance, was St. Louis, established as a trading post on the richly wooded bluffs opposite

Cahokia by Pierre Laclede in 1764.

Associated with Laclede in his fur-trading operations at the new post was a lithe young man named Pierre Chouteau. In 1846 - eighty-two years afterwards - Francis Parkman sat on the spacious veranda of Pierre Chouteau's country house near the city of St. Louis and heard from the lips of the venerable merchant stories of Pontiac, Saint-Ange, Croghan, and all the western worthies, red and white, of two full generations. "Not all the magic of a dream," the historian remarks, "nor the enchantments of an Arabian tale, could outmatch the waking realities which were to rise upon the vision of Pierre Chouteau. Where, in his youth, he had climbed the woody bluff, and looked abroad on prairies dotted with bison, he saw, with the dim eye of his old age, the land darkened for many a furlong with the clustered roofs of the western metropolis. For the silence of the wilderness, he heard the clang and turmoil of human labor, the din of congregated thousands; and where the great river rolls down through the forest, in lonely grandeur, he saw the waters lashed into foam beneath the prows of panting steamboats, flocking to the broad levee."

Pontiac's war long kept the English from taking actual possession of the western country. Meanwhile Saint-Ange, commanding the remnant of the French garrison at Fort Chartres, resisted as best he could the demands of the redskins for assistance against their common enemy and hoped daily for the appearance of an English force to relieve him his difficult position. In the spring of 1764 an English officer, Major Loftus, with a body of troops lately employed in planting English authority in "East Florida" and "West Florida," set out from New Orleans to take possession of the up-river settlements. A few miles above the mouth of the Red, however, the boats were fired on, without warning, from both banks of the stream, and many of the men were killed or wounded. The expedition retreated down the river with all possible speed. This display of faintheartedness won the keen ridicule of the French, and the Governor, D'Abadie, with mock magnanimity, offered an escort of French soldiery to protect the party on its way back to Pensacola! Within a few months a second attempt was projected, but news of the bad temper of the Indians caused the leader, Captain Pittman, to turn back after reaching New Orleans.

Baffled in this direction, the new commander-in-chief, General Gage, resolved to accomplish the desired end by an expedition from Fort Pitt. Pontiac, however, was known to be still plotting vengeance at that time, and it seemed advisable to break the way for the proposed expedition by a special mission to placate the Indians. For this delicate task Sir William Johnson selected a trader of long experience and of good standing among the western tribes, George Croghan. Notwithstanding many mishaps, the plan was carried out. With two boats and a considerable party of soldiers and friendly Delawares, Croghan left Fort Pitt in May, 1765. As he descended the Ohio he carefully plotted the river's windings and wrote out an interesting description of the fauna and flora observed. All went well until he reached the mouth of the Wabash. There the party was set upon by a band of Kickapoos, who killed half a dozen of his men. Fluent apologies were at once offered. They had made the attack, they explained, only because the French had reported that the Indians with Croghan's band were Cherokees, the Kickapoos' most deadly enemies. Now that their mistake was apparent, the artful emissaries declared, their regret was indeed deep.

All of this was sheer pretense, and Croghan and his surviving followers were kept under close guard and were carried along with the Kickapoo band up the Wabash to Vincennes, where the trader encountered old Indian friends who soundly rebuked the captors for their inhospitality. Croghan knew the Indian nature too well to attempt to thwart the plans of his "hosts." Accordingly he went out with the band to the upper Wabash post Ouiatanon, where he received deputation after deputation from the neighboring tribes, smoked pipes of peace, made speeches, and shook hands with greasy warriors by the score. Here came a messenger from Saint-Ange asking him to proceed to Fort Chartres. Here, also, Pontiac met him, and, after being assured that the English had no intention of enslaving the natives, declared that he would no longer stand in the conquerors' path. Though in unexpected manner, Croghan's mission was accomplished, and, with many evidences of favor from the natives, he went on to Detroit and thence to Niagara, where he reported to Johnson that the situation in the West was ripe for the establishment of English sovereignty.

There was no reason for further delay, and Captain Thomas Sterling was dispatched with a hundred Highland veterans to take ever the settlements. Descending the Ohio from Fort Pitt, the expedition reached Fort Chartres just as the frosty air began to presage the coming of winter. On October 10, 1765, - more than two and a half years after the signing of the Treaty of Paris, - Saint-Ange made the long-desired transfer of authority. General Gage's high-sounding proclamation was read, the British flag was run up, and

Sterling's red-coated soldiery established itself in the citadel. In due time small detachments were sent to Vincennes and other posts; and the triumph of the British power over Frenchman and Indian was complete. Saint-Ange retired with his little garrison to St. Louis, where, until the arrival of a Spanish lieutenant-governor in 1770, he acted by common consent as chief magistrate.

The creoles who passed under the English flag suffered little from the change. Their property and trading interests were not molested, and the English commandants made no effort to displace the old laws and usages. Documents were written and records were kept in French as well as English. The village priest and the notary retained their accustomed places of paternal authority. The old idyllic life went on. Population increased but little; barter, hunting, and trapping still furnished the means of a simple subsistence; and with music, dancing, and holiday festivities the lighthearted populace managed to crowd more pleasure into a year than the average English frontiersman got in a lifetime.

For a year or two after the European pacification of 1763 Indian disturbances held back the flood of settlers preparing to enter, through the Alleghany passes, the upper valleys of the westward flowing rivers. Neither Indian depredations nor proclamations of kings, however, could long interpose an effectual restraint. The supreme object of the settlers was to obtain land. Formerly there was land enough for all along the coasts or in the nearer uplands. But population, as Franklin computed, was doubling in twenty-five years; vacant areas had already been occupied; and desirable lands had been gathered into great speculative holdings. Newcomers were consequently forced to cross the mountains - and not only newcomers, but all residents who were still land-hungry and ambitious to better their condition.

To such the appeal of the great West was irresistible. The English Government might indeed regard the region as a "barren waste" or a "profitless wilderness," but not so the Scotch-Irish, Huguenot, and Palatine homeseekers who poured by the thousands through the Chesapeake and Delaware ports. Pushing past the settled seaboard country, these rugged men of adventure plunged joyously into the forest depths and became no less the founders of the coming nation than were the Pilgrims and the Cavaliers.

Ahead of the home-builder, however, went the speculator. It has been remarked that "from the time when Joliet and La Salle first found their way into the heart of the great West up to the present day when far-off Alaska is in the throes of development, 'big business' has been engaged in western speculation."* In pre-revolutionary days this speculation took the form of procuring, by grant or purchase, large tracts of western land which were to be sold and colonized at a profit. Franklin was interested in a number of such projects. Washington, the Lees, and a number of other prominent Virginians were connected with an enterprise which absorbed the old Ohio Company; and in 1770 Washington, piloted by Croghan, visited the Ohio country with a view to the discovery of desirable areas. Eventually he acquired western holdings amounting to thirty-three thousand acres, with a water-front of sixteen miles on the Ohio and of forty miles on the Great Kanawha.

* Alvord, Mississippi Valley in "British Politics," vol. I, p.86.

In 1773 a company promoted by Samuel Wharton, Benjamin Franklin, William Johnson, and a London banker, Thomas Walpole, secured the grant of two and a half million acres between the Alleghanies and the Ohio, which was to be the seat of a colony called Vandalia. This departure from the policy laid down in the Proclamation of 1763 was made reluctantly, but with a view to giving a definite western limit to the seaboard provinces. The Government's purpose was fully understood in America, and the project was warmly opposed, especially by Virginia, the chartered claimant of the territory. The early outbreak of the Revolutionary War wrecked the project, and nothing ever came of it - or indeed of any colonization proposal contemporary with it. By and large, the building of the West was to be the work, not of colonizing companies or other corporate interests, but of individual homeseekers, moving into the new country on their own responsibility and settling where and when their own interests and inclinations led.

Chapter III.

The Revolution Begins

One of the grievances given prominence in the Declaration of Independence was that the English Crown had "abolished the free system of English laws in a neighbouring province, establishing therein an arbitrary government, and enlarging its boundaries so as to render it at once an example and fit instrument for introducing the same arbitrary rule into these colonies." The measure which was in the minds of the signers was the Quebec Act of 1774; and the feature to which they especially objected was the extension of this peculiarly governed Canadian province to include the whole of the territory north of the Ohio and east of the Mississippi.

The Quebec Act was passed primarily to remedy a curious mistake made by King George's ministers eleven years earlier. The Proclamation of 1763 had been intended to apply to the new French speaking possessions in only a general way, leaving matters of government and law to be regulated at a later date. But through oversight it ordained the establishment of English law, and even of a representative assembly, precisely as in the other new provinces. The English governors were thus put in an awkward position. They were required to introduce English political forms and legal practices. Yet the inexperience and suspicion of the people made it unwise, if not impossible, to do so. When, for example, jury trial was broached, the peasants professed to be quite unable to understand why the English should prefer to have matters of law decided by tailors and shoemakers rather than by a judge; and as for a legislature, they frankly confessed that assemblies "had drawn upon other colonies so much distress, and had occasioned so much riot and bloodshed, that they had hoped never to have one."

The Act of 1774 relieved the situation by restoring French law in civil affairs, abolishing jury trial except in criminal cases, rescinding the grant of representative government, and confirming the Catholic clergy in the rights and privileges which they hard enjoyed under the old regime. This would have aroused no great amount of feeling among New Englanders and Virginians if the new arrangements had been confined to the bounds of the original province. But they were not so restricted. On the contrary, the new province was made to include the great region between the Alleghanies and the Mississippi, southward to the Ohio; and it was freely charged that a principal object of the English Government was to sever the West from the shore colonies and permanently link it with the St. Lawrence Valley rather than with the Atlantic slope.

At all events, the Quebec Act marked the beginning of civil government in the great Northwest. On November 9, 1775, Henry Hamilton appeared as Lieutenant-Governor at the new capital, Detroit. Already the "shot heard round the world" had been fired by the farmers at Lexington; and Hamilton had been obliged to thread his way through General Montgomery's lines about Montreal in the guise of a Canadian. Arrived at his new seat of authority, he found a pleasant, freshly fortified town whose white population had grown to fifteen hundred, including a considerable number of English-speaking settlers. The country round was overrun with traders, who cheated and cajoled the Indians without conscience; the natives, in turn, were a nondescript lot, showing in pitiful manner the bad effects of their contact with the whites.

As related by a contemporary chronicler - a Pennsylvanian who lived for years among the western tribes - an Indian hunting party on arriving at Detroit would trade perhaps a third of the peltries which they brought in for fine clothes, ammunition, paint, tobacco, and like articles. Then a keg of brandy would be purchased, and a council would be held to decide who was to get drunk and who to keep sober. All arms and clubs were taken away and hidden, and the orgy would begin. It was the task of those who kept sober to prevent the drunken ones from killing one another, a task always hazardous and frequently unsuccessful, sometimes as many as five being killed in a night. When the keg was empty, brandy was brought by the kettleful and ladled out with large wooden spoons; and this was kept up until the last skin had been disposed of. Then, dejected, wounded, lamed, with their fine new shirts torn, their blankets burned, and with nothing but their ammunition and tobacco saved, they would start off down the river to hunt in the Ohio country and begin again the same round of alternating toil and debauchery. In the history of the country there is hardly a more depressing chapter than that which records the easy descent of the red man, once his taste for "fire water" was developed, to bestiality and impotence.

The coming on of the Revolution produced no immediate effects in the West. The meaning of the occurrences round Boston was but slowly grasped by the frontier folk. There was little indeed that the Westerners could do to help the cause of the eastern patriots, and most of them, if left alone, would have been only distant spectators of the conflict. But orders given to the British agents and commanders called for the ravaging of the trans-Alleghany country; and as a consequence the West became an important theater of hostilities.

The British agents had no troops with which to undertake military operations on a considerable scale, but they had one great resource - the Indians - and this they used with a reckless disregard of all considerations of humanity. In the summer of 1776 the Cherokees were furnished with fifty horse-loads of ammunition and were turned loose upon the back country of Georgia and the Carolinas. Other tribes were prompted to depredations farther north. White, half-breed, and Indian agents went through the forests inciting the natives to deeds of horror; prices were fixed on scalps - and it is significant of the temper of these agents that a woman's scalp was paid for as readily as a man's.

In every corner of the wilderness the bloody scenes of Pontiac's war were now reenacted. Bands of savages lurked about the settlements, ready to attack at any unguarded moment; and wherever the thin blue smoke of a settler's cabin rose, prowlers lay in wait. A woman might not safely go a hundred yards to milk a cow, or a man lead a horse to water. The farmer carried a gun strapped to his side as he ploughed, and he scarcely dared venture into the woods for the winter's supply of fuel and game. Hardly a day passed on which a riderless horse did not come galloping into some lonely clearing, telling of afresh tragedy on the trail.

The rousing of the Indians against the frontiersmen was an odious act. The people of the back country were in not the slightest degree responsible for the revolt against British authority in the East. They were non-combatants, and no amount of success in sweeping them from their homes could affect the larger outcome. The crowning villainy of this shameful policy was the turning of the redskins loose to prey upon helpless women and children.

The responsibility for this inhumanity must be borne in some degree by the government of George III. "God and nature," wrote the Earl of Suffolk piously, "hath put into our hands the scalping-knife and tomahawk, to torture them into unconditional submission." But the fault lay chiefly with the British officers at the western posts - most of all, with Lieutenant-Governor Hamilton at Detroit. Probably no British representative in America was on better terms with the natives. He drank with them, sang war-songs with them, and received them with open arms when they came in from the forests with the scalps of white men dangling at their belts. A great council on the banks of the Detroit in June, 1778, was duly opened with prayer, after which Hamilton harangued the assembled Chippewas, Hurons, Mohawks, and Potawatomi on their "duties" in the war and congratulated them on the increasing numbers of their prisoners and scalps, and then urged them to redoubled activity by holding out the prospect of the complete expulsion of white men from the great interior hunting-grounds.

Scarcely were the deputations attending this council well on their way homewards when a courier arrived from the Illinois country bringing startling news. The story was that a band of three hundred rebels led by one George Rogers Clark had fallen upon the Kaskaskia settlements, had thrown the commandant into irons, and had exacted from the populace an oath of allegiance to the Continental Congress. It was reported, too, that Cahokia had been taken, and that, even as the messenger was leaving Kaskaskia, "Gibault, a French priest, had his horse ready saddled to go to Vincennes to receive the submission of the inhabitants in the name of the rebels."

George Rogers Clark was a Virginian, born in the foothills of Albemarle County three years before Braddock's defeat. His family was not of the landed gentry, but he received some education, and then, like Washington and many other adventuresome young men of the day, became a surveyor. At the age of twenty-two he was a member of Governor Dunmore's staff. During a surveying expedition he visited Kentucky, which so pleased him that in 1774 he decided to make that part of the back country his home. He was even then a man of powerful frame, with broad brow, keen blue eyes, and a dash of red in his hair from a Scottish ancestress - a man, too, of ardent patriotism, strong common sense, and exceptional powers of initiative and leadership. Small wonder that in the rapidly developing commonwealth beyond the mountains he quickly became a dominating spirit.

With a view to organizing a civil government and impressing upon the Virginia authorities the need of defending the western settlements, the men of

Kentucky held a convention at Harrodsburg in the spring of 1775 and elected two delegates to present their petition to the Virginia Assembly. Clark was one of them. The journey to Williamsburg was long and arduous, and the delegates arrived only to find that the Legislature had adjourned. The visit, none the less, gave Clark an opportunity to explain to the new Governor - "a certain Patrick Henry, of Hanover County," as the royalist Dunmore contemptuously styled his successor - the situation in the back country and to obtain five hundred pounds of powder. He also induced the authorities to take steps which led to the definite organization of Kentucky as a county of Virginia.

In the bloody days that followed, most of the pioneers saw nothing to be done except to keep close guard and beat off the Indians when they came. A year or two of that sort of desperate uncertainty gave Clark an idea. Why not meet the trouble at its source by capturing the British posts and suppressing the commandants whose orders were mainly responsible for the atrocities? There was just one obstacle: Kentucky could spare neither men nor money for the undertaking.

In the spring of 1777 two young hunters, disguised as traders, were dispatched to the Illinois country and to the neighborhood of Vincennes, to spy out the land. They brought back word that the posts were not heavily manned, and that the French-speaking population took little interest in the war and was far from reconciled to British rule. The prospect seemed favorable. Without making his purpose known to anyone, Clark forthwith joined a band of disheartened settlers and made his way with them over the Wilderness Trail to Virginia. By this time a plan on the part of the rebels for the defense of the Kentucky settlements had grown into a scheme for the conquest of the whole Northwest.

Clark's proposal came opportunely. Burgoyne's surrender had given the colonial cause a rosy hue, and already the question of the occupation of the Northwest had come up for discussion in Congress. Governor Henry thought well of the plan. He called Thomas Jefferson, George Mason, and George Wythe into conference, and on January 2, 1778, Clark was given two sets of orders - one, for publication, commissioning him to raise seven companies of fifty men each "in any county of the Commonwealth" for militia duty in Kentucky, the other, secret, authorizing him to use this force in an expedition for the capture of the "British post at Kaskasky." To meet the costs, only twelve hundred pounds in depreciated continental currency could be raised. But the Governor and his friends promised to try to secure three hundred acres of land for each soldier, in case the project should succeed. The strictest secrecy was preserved, and, even if the Legislature had been in session, the project would probably not have been divulged to it.

Men and supplies were gathered at Fort Pitt and Wheeling and were carried down the Ohio to "the Falls," opposite the site of Louisville. The real object of the expedition was concealed until this point was reached. On learning of the project, the men were surprised, and some refused to go farther. But in a few weeks one hundred and seventy-five men, organized in four companies, were in readiness. The start was made on the 24th of June. Just as the little flotilla of clumsy flatboats was caught by the rapid current, the landscape was darkened by an eclipse of the sun. The superstitious said that this was surely an evil omen. But Clark was no believer in omens, and he ordered the bateaux to proceed. He had lately received news of the French alliance, and was surer than ever that the habitants would make common cause with his forces and give him complete success.

To appear on the Mississippi was to run the risk of betraying the object of the expedition to the defenders of the posts. Hence the wily commander decided to make the last stages of his advance by an overland route. At the deserted site of Fort Massac, nine miles below the mouth of the Tennessee, the little army left the Ohio and struck off northwest on a march of one hundred and twenty miles, as the crow flies, across the tangled forests and rich prairies of southern Illinois.

Six days brought the invaders to the Kaskaskia River, three miles above the principal settlement. Stealing silently along the bank of the stream on the night of the 4th of July, they crossed in boats which they seized at a farmhouse and arrived at the palisades wholly unobserved. Half of the force was stationed in the form of a cordon, so that no one might escape. The remainder followed Clark through an unguarded gateway into the village.

According to a story long current, the officials of the post were that night giving a ball, and all of the elite, not of Kaskaskia alone but of the neighboring settlements as well, were joyously dancing in one of the larger rooms of the fort. Leaving his men some paces distant, Clark stepped to the entrance of the hall, and for some time leaned unobserved against the doorpost, grimly watching the gayety. Suddenly the air was rent by a warwhoop which brought the dancers to a stop. An Indian brave, lounging in the firelight, had caught a glimpse of the tall, gaunt, buff and blue figure in the doorway and had recognized it. Women shrieked; men cursed; the musicians left their posts; all was disorder. Advancing, Clark struck a theatrical pose and in a voice of command told the merrymakers to go on with their dancing, but to take note that they now danced, not as subjects of King George but as Virginians. Finding that they were in no mood for further diversion, he sent them to their homes; and all night they shivered with fear, daring not so much as to light a candle lest they should be set upon and murdered in their beds.

This account is wholly unsupported by contemporary testimony, and it probably sprang from the imagination of some good frontier story-teller. It contains at least this much truth, that the settlement, after being thrown into panic, was quickly and easily taken. Curiously enough, the commandant was a Frenchman, Rocheblave, who had thriftily entered the British service. True to the trust reposed in him, he protested and threatened, but to no avail. The garrison, now much diminished, was helpless, and the populace - British, French, and Indian alike - was not disposed to court disaster by offering armed resistance. Hence, on the morning after the capture the oath of fidelity was administered, and the American flag was hoisted for the first time within view of the Father of Waters. After dispatching word to General Carleton that he had been compelled to surrender the post to "the self-styled Colonel, Mr. Clark," Rocheblave was sent as a captive to Williamsburg, where he soon broke parole and escaped. His slaves were sold for five hundred pounds, and the money was distributed among the troops. Cahokia was occupied without resistance, and the

French priest, Father Pierre Gibault, whose parish extended from Lake Superior to the Ohio, volunteered to go to Vincennes and win its inhabitants to the American cause.

Like Kaskaskia and Cahokia, the Wabash settlement had been put in charge of a commandant of French descent. The village, however, was at the moment without a garrison, and its chief stronghold, Fort Sackville, was untenanted. Gibault argued forcefully for acceptance of American sovereignty, and within two days the entire population filed into the little church and took the oath of allegiance. The astonished Indians were given to understand that their former "Great Father," the King of France, had returned to life, and that they must comply promptly with his wishes or incur his everlasting wrath for having given aid to the despised British.

Thus without the firing of a shot or the shedding of a drop of blood, the vast Illinois and Wabash country was won for the future United States. Clark's plan was such that its success was assured by its very audacity. It never occurred to the British authorities that their far western forts were in danger, and they were wholly unprepared to fly to the defense of such distant posts. British sovereignty on the Mississippi was never recovered; and in the autumn of 1778 Virginia took steps to organize her new conquest by setting up the county of Illinois, which included all her territories lying "on the western side of the Ohio."

Chapter IV.

The Conquest Completed

Lieutenant-Governor Hamilton had many faults, but sloth was not one of them; and when he heard what had happened he promptly decided to regain the posts and take the upstart Kentucky conqueror captive. Emissaries were sent to the Wabash country to stir up the Indians, and for weeks the Detroit settlement resounded with preparations for the expedition. Boats were built or repaired, guns were cleaned, ammunition was collected in boxes, provisions were put up in kegs or bags, baubles for the Indians were made or purchased. Cattle and wheels, together with a six-pounder, were sent ahead to be in readiness for use at various stages of the journey.

Further weeks were consumed in awaiting reenforcements which never came; and in early October, when the wild geese were scudding southward before the first snow flurries of the coming winter, the commandant started for the reconquest with a motley force of thirty-six British regulars, forty-five local volunteers, seventy-nine local militia, and sixty Indians. Reenforcements were gathered on the road, so that when Vincennes was reached the little army numbered about five hundred. From Detroit the party dropped easily down the river to Lake Erie, where it narrowly escaped destruction in a blinding snowstorm. By good management, however, it was brought safely to the Maumee, up whose sluggish waters the bateaux were laboriously poled. A portage of nine miles gave access to the Wabash. Here the water was very shallow, and only by building occasional dikes to produce a current did the party find it possible to complete the journey. As conferences with the Indians further delayed them, it was not until a few days before Christmas that the invaders reached their goal.

The capture of Vincennes proved easy enough. The surrender, none the less, was made in good military style. There were two iron three-pounders in the wretched little fort, and one of these was loaded to the muzzle and placed in the open gate. As Hamilton and his men advanced, so runs a not very well authenticated story, Lieutenant Helm stood by the gun with a lighted taper and called sternly upon the invaders to halt. The British leader demanded the surrender of the garrison. Helm parleyed and asked for terms. Hamilton finally conceded the honors of war, and Helm magnanimously accepted. Hamilton thereupon drew up his forces in a double line, the British on one side and the Indians on the other; and the garrison - one officer and one soldier - solemnly marched out between them! After the "conquerors" had regained their equanimity, the cross of St. George was once more run up on the fort. A body of French militia returned to British allegiance with quite as much facility as it had shown in accepting American sovereignty under the eloquence of Father Gibault; and the French inhabitants, gathered again in the church, with perfectly straight faces acknowledged that they had "sinned against God and man" by taking sides with the rebels, and promised to be loyal thereafter to George III.

Had the British forces immediately pushed on, this same scene might have been repeated at Kaskaskia and Cahokia. Clark's position there was far from strong. Upon the expiration of their term of enlistment most of his men had gone back to Kentucky or Virginia, and their places had been taken mainly by creoles, whose steadfastness was doubtful. Furthermore, the Indians were restless, and it was only by much vigilance and bravado that they were kept in a respectful mood. All this was well known to Hamilton, who now proposed to follow up the recapture of the Mississippi posts by the obliteration of all traces of American authority west of the Alleghanies.

The difficulties and dangers of a midwinter campaign in the flooded Illinois country were not to be lightly regarded, and weeks of contending with icy blasts and drenching rains lent a seat by an open fire unusual attractiveness. Hence the completion of the campaign was postponed until spring - a decision which proved the salvation of the American cause in the West. As means of subsistence were slender, most of the Detroit militia were sent home, and the Indians were allowed to scatter to their distant wigwams. The force kept at the post numbered only about eighty or ninety whites, with a few Indians.

Clark now had at Kaskaskia a band of slightly over a hundred men. He understood Hamilton's army to number five or six hundred. The outlook was dubious, until Francois Vigo, a friendly Spanish trader of St. Louis, escaping captivity at Vincennes, came to Kaskaskia with the information that Hamilton had sent away most of his troops; and this welcome news gave the doughty Kentuckian a brilliant idea. He would defend his post by attacking the invaders while they were yet at Vincennes, and before they were ready to resume operations. "The case is desperate," he wrote to Governor Henry, "but, sir, we must either quit the country or attack Mr. Hamilton." He had probably never heard of Scipio Africanus but, like that indomitable Roman, he proposed to carry the war straight into the enemy's country. "There were undoubtedly appalling difficulties," says Mr. Roosevelt, "in the way of a midwinter march and attack; and the fact that Clark attempted and performed the feat which Hamilton dared not try, marks just the difference between a man of genius and a good, brave, ordinary commander."

Preparations were pushed with all speed. A large, flat-bottomed boat, the Willing, was fitted out with four guns and was sent down the Mississippi with forty men to ascend the Ohio and the Wabash to a place of rendezvous not far from the coveted post. By early February the depleted companies were recruited to their full strength; and after the enterprise had been solemnly blessed by Father Gibault, Clark and his forces, numbering one hundred and thirty men, pushed out upon the desolate, windswept prairie.

The distance to be covered was about two hundred and thirty miles. Under favorable circumstances, the trip could have been made in five or six days and with little hardship. The rainy season, however, was now at its height, and the country was one vast quagmire, overrun by swollen streams which could be crossed only at great risk. Ten days of wearisome marching brought the expedition to the forks of the Little Wabash. The entire region between the two channels was under water, and for a little time it looked as if the whole enterprise would have to be given up. There were no boats; provisions were running low; game was scarce; and fires could not be built for cooking.

But Clark could not be turned back by such difficulties. He plunged ahead of his men, struck tip songs and cheers to keep them in spirit, played the buffoon, went wherever danger was greatest, and by an almost unmatched display of bravery, tact, and firmness, won the redoubled admiration of his suffering followers and held them together. Murmurs arose among the creoles, but the Americans showed no signs of faltering. For more than a week the party floundered through the freezing water, picked its way from one outcropping bit of earth to another, and seldom found opportunity to eat or sleep. Rifles and powder-horns had to be borne by the hour above the soldiers' heads to keep them dry.

Finally, on the 23d of February, a supreme effort carried the troops across the Horseshoe Plain, breast-deep in water, and out upon high ground two miles from Vincennes. By this time many of the men were so weakened that they could drag themselves along only with assistance. But buffalo meat and corn were confiscated from the canoes of some passing squaws, and soon the troops were refreshed and in good spirits. The battle with the enemy ahead seemed as nothing when compared with the struggle with the elements which they had successfully waged. No exploit of the kind in American history surpasses this, unless it be Benedict Arnold's winter march through the wilderness of Maine in 1775 to attack Quebec.

Two or three creole hunters were now taken captive,

and from them Clark learned that no one in Vincennes knew of his approach. They reported, however, that, although the habitants were tired of the "Hair-Buyer's" presence and would gladly return to American allegiance, some two hundred Indians had just arrived at the fort. The Willing had not been heard from. But an immediate attack seemed the proper course; and the young colonel planned and carried it out with the curious mixture of bravery and braggadocio of which he was a past master.

First he drew up a lordly letter, addressed to the inhabitants of the town, and dispatched it by one of his creole prisoners. "Gentlemen," it ran, "being now within two miles of your village with my army...and not being willing to surprise you, I take this step to request such of you as are true citizens, and willing to enjoy the liberty I bring you, to remain still in your houses. And those, if any there be, that are friends to the King, will instantly repair to the fort and join the Hair-Buyer General and fight like men." Having thus given due warning, he led his "army" forward, marching and counter-marching his meager forces among the trees and hills to give an appearance of great numbers, while he and his captains helped keep up the illusion by galloping wildly here and there on horses they had confiscated, as if ordering a vast array. At nightfall the men advanced upon the stockade and opened fire from two directions.

Not until a sergeant reeled from his chair with a bullet in his breast did the garrison realize that it was really under attack. The habitants had kept their secret well. There was a beating of drums and a hurrying to arms, and throughout the night a hot fusillade was kept up. By firing from behind houses and trees, and from rifle pits that were dug before the attack began, the Americans virtually escaped loss; while Hamilton's gunners were picked off as fast as they appeared at the portholes of the fort. Clark's ammunition ran low, but the habitants furnished a fresh supply and at the same time a hot breakfast for the men. In a few hours the cannon were silenced, and parleys were opened. Hamilton insisted that he and his garrison were "not disposed to be awed into an action unworthy of British subjects," but they were plainly frightened, and Clark finally sent the commandant back to the fort from a conference in the old French church with the concession of one hour's time in which to decide what he would do. To help him make up his mind, the American leader caused half a dozen Indians who had just returned from the forests with white men's scalps dangling at their belts to be tomahawked and thrown into the river within plain view of the garrison.

Surrender promptly followed. Hamilton and twenty-five of his men were sent off as captives to Virginia, where the commandant languished in prison until, in 1780, he was paroled at the suggestion of Washington. On taking, an oath of neutrality, the remaining British sympathizers were set at liberty. For a second time the American flag floated over Indiana soil, not again to be lowered.

Immediately after the capitulation of Hamilton, a scouting-party captured a relief expedition which was on its way from Detroit and placed in Clark's hands ten thousand pounds' worth of supplies for distribution as prize-money among his deserving men. The commander's cup of satisfaction was filled to the brim when the Willing appeared with a long-awaited messenger from Governor Henry who brought to the soldiers the thanks of the Legislature of Virginia for the capture of Kaskaskia and also the promise of more substantial reward.

The whole of the Illinois and Indiana country was now in American hands. Tenure, however, was precarious so long as Detroit remained a British stronghold, and Clark now broadened his plans to embrace the capture of that strategic place. Leaving Vincennes in charge of a garrison of forty men, he returned to Kaskaskia with the Willing and set about organizing a new expedition. Kentucky pledged three hundred men, and Virginia promised to help. But when, in midsummer, the commander returned to Vincennes to consolidate and organize his force, he found the numbers to be quite insufficient. From Kentucky there came only thirty men.

Disappointment followed disappointment; he was ordered to build a fort at the mouth of the Ohio - a project of which be had himself approved; and when at last he had under his command a force that might have been adequate for the Detroit expedition, he was obliged to use it in meeting a fresh incursion of savages which had been stirred up by the new British commandant on the Lakes. But Thomas Jefferson, who in 1779 succeeded Henry as Governor of Virginia, was deeply interested in the Detroit project, and at his suggestion Washington gave Clark an order on the commandant of Fort Pitt for guns, supplies, and such troops as could be spared. On January 22, 1781, Jefferson appointed Clark "brigadier-general of the forces to be embodied on an expedition westward of the Ohio." Again Clark was doomed to disappointment.

One obstacle after another interposed. Yet as late as May, 1781, the expectant conqueror wrote to Washington that he had "not yet lost sight of Detroit." Suitable opportunity for the expedition never came, and when peace was declared the northern stronghold was still in British hands.

Clark's later days were clouded. Although Virginia gave him six thousand acres of land in southern Indiana and presented him with a sword, peace left him without employment, and he was never able to adjust himself to the changed situation. For many years he lived alone in a little cabin on the banks of the Ohio, spending his time hunting, fishing,and brooding over the failure of Congress to reward him in more substantial manner for his services. He was land-poor, lonely, and embittered. In 1818 he died a paralyzed and helpless cripple. His resting place is in Cave Hill Cemetery, Louisville; the finest statue of him stands in Monument Circle, Indianapolis - "an athletic figure, scarcely past youth, tall and sinewy, with a drawn sword, in an attitude of energetic encouragement, as if getting his army through the drowned lands of the Wabash."*

* Hosmer, "Short History of the Mississippi Valley." p. 94.

The capture of Vincennes determined the fate of the Northwest. Frontier warfare nevertheless went steadily on. In 1779 Spain entered the contest as an ally of France, and it became the object of the British commanders on the Lakes not only to recover the posts lost to the Americans but to seize St. Louis and other Spanish strongholds on the west bank of the Mississippi. In 1780 Lieutenant-Governor Patrick

Sinclair, a bustling, garrulous old soldier stationed at Michilimackinac, sent a force of some nine hundred traders, servants, and Indians down the Mississippi to capture both the American and Spanish settlements. An attack on St. Louis failed, as did likewise a series of efforts against Cahokia and Kaskaskia, and the survivors were glad to reach their northern headquarters again, with nothing to show for their pains except a dozen prisoners.

Not to be outdone, the Spanish commandant at St. Louis sent an expedition to capture British posts in the Lake country. An arduous winter march brought the avengers and their Indian allies to Fort St. Joseph, a mile or two west of the present city of Niles, Michigan. It would be ungracious to say that this post was selected for attack because it was without a garrison. At all events, the place was duly seized, the Spanish standard was set up, and possession of "the fort and its dependencies" was taken in the name of his Majesty Don Carlos III. No effort was made to hold the settlement permanently, and the British from Detroit promptly retook it. Probably the sole intention had been to add somewhat to the strength of the Spanish position at the forthcoming negotiations for peace.

The war in the West ended, as it began, in a carnival of butchery. Treacherous attacks, massacres, burnings, and pillagings were everyday occurrences, and white men were hardly less at fault than red. Indeed the most discreditable of all the recorded episodes of the time was a heartless massacre by Americans of a large band of Indians that had been Christianized by Moravian missionaries and brought together in a peaceful community on the Muskingum. This slaughter of the innocents at Gnadenhutten ("the Tents of Grace") reveals the frontiersman at his worst. But it was dearly paid for. From the Lakes to the Gulf redskins rose for vengeance. Villages were wiped out, and murderous bands swept far into Virginia and Pennsylvania, evading fortified posts in order to fall with irresistible fury on unsuspecting traders and settlers.

In midsummer, 1782, news of the cessation of hostilities between Great Britain and her former seaboard colonies reached the back country, and the commandant at Detroit made an honest effort to stop all offensive operations. A messenger failed, however, to reach a certain Captain Caldwell, operating in the Ohio country, in time to prevent him from attacking a Kentucky settlement and bringing on the deadly Battle of Blue Licks, in which the Americans were defeated with a loss of seventy-one men. George Rogers Clark forthwith led a retaliatory expedition against the Miami towns, taking prisoners, recapturing whites, and destroying British trading establishments; and with this final flare-up the Revolution came to an end in the Northwest.

The soldier had won the back country for the new nation. Could the diplomat hold it? As early as March 19, 1779, - just three weeks after Clark's capture of Vincennes, - the Continental Congress formally laid claim to the whole of the Northwest; and a few months later John Adams was instructed to negotiate for peace on the understanding that the country's northern and western boundaries were to be the line of the Great Lakes and the Mississippi. When, in 1781, Franklin, Jefferson, Jay, and Laurens were appointed to assist Adams in the negotiation, the new Congress of the Confederation stated that the earlier instructions on boundaries represented its "desires and expectations."

It might have been supposed that if Great Britain could be brought to accept these terms there would be no further difficulty. But obstacles arose from other directions. France had entered the war for her own reasons, and looked with decidedly more satisfaction on the defeat of Great Britain than on the prospect of a new and powerful nation in the Western Hemisphere. Furthermore, she was in close alliance with Spain; and Spain had no sympathy whatever with the American cause as such. At all events, she did not want the United States for a neighbor on the Mississippi.

The American commissioners were under instructions to make no peace without consulting France. But when, in the spring of 1782, Jay came upon the scene of the negotiations at Paris, he demurred. He had been for some time in Spain, and he carried to Paris not only a keen contempt for the Spanish people and Spanish politics, but a strong suspicion that Spain was using her influence to keep the United States from getting the territory between the Lakes and the Ohio. France soon fell under similar suspicion, for she was under obligations, as everyone knew, to satisfy Spain; and little time elapsed before the penetrating American diplomat was semiofficially assured that his suspicions in both directions were well founded.

The mainspring of Spanish policy was the desire to make the Gulf of Mexico a closed sea, under exclusive Spanish control. This plan would be frustrated if the Americans acquired an outlet on the Gulf; furthermore, it would be jeopardized if they retained control on the upper Mississippi. Hence, the States must be kept back from the great river; safety dictated that they be confined to the region east of the Appalachians.

An ingenious plan was thereupon developed. Spain was to resume possession of the Floridas, insuring thereby the coveted unbroken coast line on the Gulf. The vast area between the Mississippi and the Appalachians and south of the Ohio was to be an Indian territory, half under Spanish and half under American "protection." The entire region north of the Ohio was to be kept by Great Britain, or, at the most, divided - on lines to be determined - between Great Britain and the United States. From Rayneval, confidential secretary of the French foreign minister Vergennes, Jay learned that the French Government proposed to give this scheme its support.

Had such terms as these been forced on the new nation, the hundreds of Virginian and Pennsylvanian pioneers who had given up their lives in the planting of American civilization in the back country would have turned in their graves. But Jay had no notion of allowing the scheme to succeed. He sent an emissary to England to counteract the Spanish and French influence. He converted Adams to his way of thinking, and even raised doubts in Franklin's mind. Finally he induced his colleagues to cast their instructions to the winds and negotiate a treaty with the mother country independently.

This simplified matters immensely. Great Britain was a beaten nation, and from the beginning her commissioners played a losing game. There was much haggling over the loyalists, the fisheries, debts; but the boundaries were quickly drawn. Great Britain preferred to see the disputed western country in American hands rather than to leave a chance for it to fall under the control of one of her European rivals.

Accordingly, the Treaty of Paris drew the interior boundary of the new nation through the Great Lakes and connecting waters to the Lake of the Woods; from the most northwestern point of the Lake of the Woods due west to the Mississippi (an impossible line); down the Mississippi to latitude 31 degrees; thence east, by that parallel and by the line which is now the northern boundary of Florida, to the ocean. Three nations, instead of two, again shared the North American Continent: Great Britain kept the territory north of the Lakes; Spain ruled the Floridas and everything west of the Mississippi; the United States held the remainder - an area of more than 825,000 square miles, with a population of three and one half millions.

Chapter V.

Wayne, The Scourge Of The Indians

"This federal republic," wrote the Spanish Count d'Aranda to his royal master in 1782, "is born a pigmy. A day will come when it will be a giant, even a colossus. Liberty of conscience, the facility for establishing a new population on immense lands, as well as the advantages of the new government, will draw thither farmers and artisans from all the nations."

Aranda correctly weighed the value of the country's vast stretches of free and fertile land. The history of the United States has been largely a story of the clearing of forests, the laying out of farms, the erection of homes, the construction of highways, the introduction of machinery, the building of railroads, the rise of towns and of great cities. The Germans of Wisconsin and Missouri, the Scandinavians of Minnesota and the Dakotas, the Poles and Hungarians of Chicago, the Irish and Italians of a thousand communities, attest the fact that the "farmers and artisans from all the nations" have had an honorable part in the achievement.

In laying plans for the development of the western lands the statesmanship of the evolutionary leaders was at its best. In the first place, the seven States which had some sort of title to tracts extending westward to the

Mississippi wisely yielded these claims to the nation; and thus was created a single, national domain which could be dealt with in accordance with a consistent policy. In the second place, Congress, as early as 1780, pledged the national Government to dispose of the western lands for the common benefit, and promised that they should be "settled and formed into distinct republican states, which shall become members of the federal union, and have the same rights of sovereignty, freedom; and independence as the other states."

Finally, in the Northwest Ordinance of 1787 there was mapped out a scheme of government admirably adapted to the liberty-loving, yet law-abiding, populations of the frontier. It was based on the broad principles of democracy, and it was sufficiently flexible to permit necessary changes as the scattered settlements developed into organized Territories and then into States. Geographical conditions, as well as racial inheritances, foreordained that the United States should be an expanding, colonizing nation; and it was of vital importance that wholesome precedents of territorial control should be established in the beginning. Louisiana, Florida, the Mexican accessions, Alaska, and even the newer tropical dependencies, owe much to the decisions that were reached in the organizing of the Northwest a century and a quarter ago.

The Northwest Ordinance was remarkable in that it was framed for a territory that had practically no white population and which, in a sense, did not belong to the United States at all. Back in 1768 Sir William Johnson's Treaty of Fort Stanwix had made the Ohio River the boundary between the white and red races of the West. Nobody at the close of the Revolution supposed that this division would be adhered to; the Northwest had not been won for purposes of an Indian reserve. None the less, the arrangements of 1768 were inherited, and the nation considered them binding except in so far as they were modified from time to time by new agreements. The first such agreement affecting the Northwest was concluded in 1785, through George Rogers Clark and two other commissioners, with the Wyandots, Delawares, Chippewas, and Ottawas. By it the United States acquired title to the southeastern half of the present State of Ohio, with a view to surveying the lands and raising revenue by selling them. Successive treaties during the next thirty years gradually transferred the whole of the Northwest from Indian hands to the new nation.

Officially, the United States recognized the validity of the Indian claims; but the pioneer homeseeker was not so certain to do so. From about 1775 the country south of the Ohio filled rapidly with settlers from Virginia and the Carolinas, so that by 1788 the white population beyond the Blue Ridge was believed to be considerably over one hundred thousand. For a decade the "Indian side," as the north shore was habitually called, was trodden only by occasional hunters, traders, and explorers. But after Clark's victories on the Mississippi and the Wabash, the frontiersmen grew bolder. By 1780 they began to plant camps and cabins on the rich bottom-lands of the Miamis, the Scioto, and the Muskingum; and when they heard that the British claims in the West had been formally yielded, they assumed that whatever they could take was theirs. With the technicalities of Indian claims they had not much patience. In 1785 Colonel Harmar, commanding at Fort Pitt, sent a deputation down the river to drive the intruders back. But his agents returned with the report that the Virginians and Kentuckians were moving into the forbidden country "by the forties and fifties," and that they gave every evidence of proposing to remain there. Surveyors were forthwith set to work in the "Seven Ranges," as the tract just to the west of the Pennsylvania boundary was called; and Fort Harmar was built at the mouth of the Muskingum to keep the over-ardent settlers back.

The close of the Revolution brought not only a swift revival of emigration to the West but also a remarkable outburst of speculation in western land. March 3, 1786, General Rufus Putnam and some other Continental officers met at the "Bunch of Grapes" Tavern in Boston and decided that it would be to their advantage to exchange for land in the Seven Ranges the paper certificates in which they had been paid for their military services. Accordingly an "Ohio Company" was organized, and Dr. Manasseh Cutler - "preacher, lawyer, doctor, statesman, scientist, land speculator" - was sent off to New York to push the matter in Congress. The upshot was that Congress authorized the sale of one and a half million acres east of the Scioto to the Ohio Company, and five million acres to a newly organized Scioto Company.

The Scioto Company fell into financial difficulties and, after making an attempt to build up a French colony at Gallipolis, collapsed. But General Putnam and his associates kept their affairs well in hand and succeeded in planting the first legal white settlement in the present State of Ohio. An arduous winter journey brought the first band of forty-eight settlers, led by Putnam himself, to the mouth of the Muskingum on April 7, 1788. Here, in the midst of a great forest dotted with terraces, cones, and other fantastic memorials of the mound-builders, they erected a blockhouse and surrounded it with cabins. For a touch of the classical, they called the fortification the Campus Martius; to be strictly up to date, they named the town Marietta, after Marie Antoinette, Queen of France. In July the little settlement was honored by being made the residence of the newly arrived Governor of the Territory, General Arthur St. Clair. Before the close of the year Congress sold one million acres between the two Miamis to Judge Symmes of New Jersey; and three little towns were at once laid out. To one of them a pedantic schoolmaster gave the name L-os-anti-ville, "the town opposite the mouth of the Licking." The name may have required too much explanation; at all events, when, in 1790, the Governor transferred the capital thither from Marietta, he rechristened the place Cincinnati, in honor of the famous Revolutionary society to which he belonged.

Land speculators are confirmed optimists. But Putnam, Cutler, Symmes, and their associates were correct in believing that the Ohio country was at the threshold of a period of remarkable development. There was one serious obstacle - the Indians. Repeated expeditions from Kentucky had pushed most of the tribes northward to the headwaters of the Miami, Scioto, and Wabash; and the Treaty of 1785 was supposed to keep them there. But it was futile to expect such an arrangement to prove lasting unless steadily backed up with force. In their squalid villages in the swampy forests of northern Ohio and Indiana the redskins grew sullen and vindictive. As they saw their favorite hunting-grounds slipping from their grasp, those who had taken part in the cession repented their generosity, while those who had no part in it pronounced it fraudulent and refused to consider themselves bound by it. Swiftly the idea took hold that the oncoming wave must be rolled back before it was too late. "White man shall not plant corn north of the Ohio" became the rallying cry.

Back of this rebelliousness lay a certain amount of British influence. The Treaty of 1783 was signed in as kindly spirit as the circumstances would permit, but its provisions were not carried out in a charitable manner. On account of alleged shortcomings of the United States, the British Government long refused to give up possession of eight or ten fortified posts in the north and west. One of these was Detroit; and the officials stationed there systematically encouraged the hordes of redskins who had congregated about the western end of Lake Erie to make all possible resistance to the American advance. The British no longer had any claim to the territories south of the Lakes, but they wanted to keep their ascendancy over the northwestern Indians, and especially to prevent the rich fur trade from falling into American hands. Ammunition and other supplies were lavished on the restless tribes. The post officials insisted that these were merely the gifts which had regularly been made in times of peace. But they were used with deadly effect against the Ohio frontiersmen; and there can be little doubt that they were intended so to be used.

By 1789 the situation was very serious. Marauding expeditions were growing in frequency; and a scout sent out by Governor St. Clair came back with the report that most of the Indians throughout the entire Northwest had "bad hearts." Washington decided that delay would be dangerous, and the nation forthwith prepared for its first war since independence. Kentucky was asked to furnish a thousand militiamen and

Pennsylvania five hundred, and the forces were ordered to come together at Fort Washington, near Cincinnati.

The rendezvous took place in the summer of 1790, and General Josiah Harmar was put in command of a punitive expedition against the Miamis. The recruits were raw, and Harmar was without the experience requisite for such an enterprise. None the less, when the little army, accompanied by three hundred regulars, and dragging three brass field-pieces, marched out of Fort Washington on a fine September day, it created a very good impression. All went well until the expedition reached the Maumee country. On the site of the present city of Fort Wayne they destroyed a number of Indian huts and burned a quantity of corn. But in a series of scattered encounters the white men were defeated, with a loss of nearly two hundred killed; and Harmar thought it the part of wisdom to retreat. He had gained nothing by the expedition; on the contrary, he had stirred the redskins to fresh aggressions, and his retreating forces were closely followed by bands of merciless raiders.

Washington knew what the effect of this reverse would be. Accordingly he called St. Clair to Philadelphia and ordered him to take personal command of a new expedition, adding a special warning against ambush and surprise. Congress aided by voting two thousand troops for six months, besides two small regiments of regulars. But everything went wrong. Recruiting proved slow; the men who were finally brought together were poor material for an army, being gathered chiefly from the streets and prisons of the seaboard cities; and supplies were shockingly inadequate.

St. Clair was a man of honest intention, but old, broken in health, and of very limited military ability; and when finally, October 4, 1791, he led his untrained forces slowly northwards from Fort Washington, he utterly failed to take measures either to keep his movements secret or to protect his men against sudden attack. The army trudged slowly through the deep forests, chopping out its own road, and rarely advancing more than five or six miles a day. The weather was favorable and game was abundant, but discontent was rife and desertions became daily occurrences. As most of the men had no taste for Indian warfare and as their pay was but two dollars a month, not all the commander's threats and entreaties could hold them in order.

On the night of the 3d of November the little army - now reduced to fourteen hundred men - camped, with divisions carelessly scattered, on the eastern fork of the Wabash, about a hundred miles north of Cincinnati and near the Indiana border. The next morning, when preparations were being made for a forced march against some Indian villages near by, a horde of redskins burst unexpectedly upon the bewildered troops, surrounded them, and threatened them with utter destruction. A brave stand was made, but there was little chance of victory. "After the first on set," as Roosevelt has described the battle, "the Indians fought in silence, no sound coming from them save the incessant rattle of their fire, as they crept from log to log, from tree to tree, ever closer and closer. The soldiers stood in close order, in the open; their musketry and artillery fire made a tremendous noise, but did little damage to a foe they could hardly see. Now and then through the hanging smoke terrible figures flitted, painted black and red, the feathers of the hawk and eagle braided in their long scalp-locks; but save for these glimpses, the soldiers knew the presence of their somber enemy only from the fearful rapidity with which their comrades fell dead and wounded in the ranks."

At last, in desperation St. Clair ordered his men to break through the deadly cordon and save themselves as best they could. The Indians kept up a hot pursuit for a distance of four miles. Then, surfeited with slaughter, they turned to plunder the abandoned camp; otherwise there would have been escape for few. As it was, almost half of the men in the engagement were killed, and less than five hundred got off with no injury. The survivors gradually straggled into the river settlements, starving and disheartened.

The page on which is written the story of St. Clair's defeat is one of the gloomiest in the history of the West. Harmar's disaster was dwarfed; not since Braddock and his regulars were cut to pieces by an unseen foe on the road to Fort Duquesne had the redskins inflicted upon their hereditary enemy a blow of such proportions. It was with a heavy heart that the Governor dispatched a messenger to Philadelphia with the news. Congress ordered an investigation; and in view of the unhappy general's high character and his courageous, though blundering, conduct during the late campaign, he was exonerated. He retained the governorship, but prudently resigned his military command.

The situation was now desperate. Everywhere the forests resounded with the exultant cries of the victors, while the British from Detroit and other posts actively encouraged the belief not only that they would furnish all necessary aid but that England herself was about to declare war on the United States. Eventually a British force from Detroit actually invaded the disputed country and built a stockade (Fort Miami) near the site of the present city of Toledo, with a view to giving the redskins convincing evidence of the seriousness of the Great White Father's intentions. Small wonder that, when St. Clair sought to obtain by diplomacy the settlement which he had failed to secure by arms, his commissioners were met with the ultimatum: "Brothers, we shall be persuaded that you mean to do us justice, if you agree that the Ohio shall remain the boundary line between us. If you will not consent thereto, our meeting will be altogether unnecessary."

It is said that Washington's first choice for the new western command was "Light-Horse Harry" Lee. But considerations of rank made the appointment inexpedient, and "Mad Anthony" Wayne was named instead. Wayne was the son of a Pennsylvania frontiersman and came honestly by his aptitude for Indian fighting. In early life he was a surveyor, and in the Revolution he won distinction as a dashing commander of Pennsylvania troops at Ticonderoga, Brandywine, Germantown, Stony Point, and other important engagements. Finally he obtained a major-general's commission in Greene's campaign in Georgia, and at the close of the war he settled in that State as a planter. His vanity - displayed chiefly in a love of fine clothes - brought upon him a good deal of criticism; and Washington, who in a Cabinet meeting characterized him as "brave and nothing else," was frankly apprehensive lest in the present business Wayne's impetuosity should lead to fresh disaster. Yet the qualities that on a dozen occasions had enabled Wayne to snatch success from almost certain defeat - alertness, decisiveness, bravery, and sheer love of hard fighting - were those now chiefly in demand.

The first task was to create an army. A few regulars were available; but most of the three or four thousand men who were needed had to be gathered wheresoever they could be found. A call for recruits brought together at Pittsburgh, in the summer of 1792, a nondescript lot of beggars, criminals, and other cast-offs of the eastern cities, no better and no worse than the adventurers who had taken service under St. Clair. Few knew anything of warfare, and on one occasion a mere report of Indians in the vicinity caused a third of the sentinels to desert their posts. But, as rigid discipline was enforced and drilling was carried on for eight and ten hours a day, by spring the survivors formed a very respectable body of troops. The scene of operations was then transferred to Fort Washington, where fresh recruits were started on a similar course of development. Profitting by the experience of his predecessors, Wayne insisted that campaigning should begin only after the troops were thoroughly prepared; and no drill-master ever worked harder to get his charges into condition for action. Going beyond the ordinary manual of arms, he taught the men to load their rifles while running at full speed, and to yell at the top of their voices while making a bayonet attack.

In October, 1793, the intrepid Major-General advanced with twenty-six hundred men into the nearer stretches of the Indian country, in order to be in a position for an advantageous spring campaign. They built Fort Greenville, eighty miles north of Cincinnati, and there spent the winter, while, on St. Clair's fatal battle-field, an advance detachment built a post which they hopefully christened Fort Recovery. Throughout the winter unending drill was kept up; and when, in June, 1794, fourteen hundred mounted militia arrived from Kentucky, Wayne found himself at the head of the largest and best-trained force that had ever been turned against the Indians west of the Alleghanies. Even before the arrival of the Kentuckians, it proved its worth by defending its forest headquarters, with practically no loss, against an attack by fifteen hundred redskins.

On the 27th of July the army moved forward in the direction of the Maumee, with closed ranks and so guarded by scouts that no chance whatever was given for surprise attacks. Washington's admonitions had been taken to heart, and the Indians could only wonder and admire. News of the army's advance traveled ahead and struck terror through the northern villages, so that many of the inhabitants fled precipitately. When the troops reached the cultivated lands about the junction of the Maumee and Auglaize rivers, they found only deserted huts and great fields of corn, from which they joyfully replenished their diminished stores. Here a fort was built and given the significant name Defiance; and from it a final offer of peace was sent out to the hostile tribes. Never doubting that the British would furnish all necessary aid, the chieftains returned evasive answers. Wayne thereupon moved his troops to the left bank of the Maumee and proceeded cautiously downstream toward the British stronghold at Fort Miami.

A few days brought the army to a place known as Fallen Timbers, where a tornado had piled the trunks and branches of mighty trees in indescribable confusion. The British post was but five or six miles distant; and there behind the breastworks which nature had provided, and in easy reach of their allies, the Indians chose to make their stand. On the morning of the 20th of August, Wayne, now so crippled by gout that he had to be lifted into his saddle, gallantly led an assault. The Indian fire was murderous, and a battalion of mounted Kentuckians was at first hurled back. But the front line of infantry rushed up and dislodged the savages from their covert, while the regular cavalry on the right charged the enemy's left flank. Before the second line of infantry could get into action the day was won. The whole engagement lasted less than three-quarters of an hour, and not a third of Wayne's three thousand men actually took part in it.

The fleeing redskins were pursued to the walls of the British fort, and even there many were slain. The British soldiery not only utterly failed to come to the relief of their hard-pressed allies, but refused to open the gates to give them shelter. The American loss was thirty-three killed and one hundred wounded. But the victory was the most decisive as yet gained over the Indians of the Northwest. A warfare of forty years was ended in as many minutes.

From the lower Maumee, Wayne marched back to Fort Defiance, and thence to the junction of the St. Mary's and St. Joseph rivers, where he built a fort and gave it the name still borne by the thriving city that grew up around it - Fort Wayne. Everywhere the American soldiers destroyed the ripened crops and burned the villages, while the terrified inhabitants fled. In November the army took up winter quarters at Fort Greenville.

At last the Americans had the upper hand. Their arms were feared; the British promises of help were no longer credited by the Indians; and it was easy for Wayne to convince the tribal representatives who visited him in large numbers during the winter that their true interest was to win the good-will of the United States. In the summer of 1795 there was a general pacification. Delegation after delegation arrived at Fort Greenville, until more than a thousand chiefs and braves were in attendance. The prestige of Wayne was still further increased when the news came that John Jay had negotiated a treaty at London under which the British posts on United States soil were finally to be given up; and on August 3rd Wayne was able to announce a great treaty wherein the natives ceded all of what is now southern Ohio and southeastern Indiana, and numerous tracts around posts within the Indian country, such as Fort Wayne, Detroit, and Michilimackinac - strategic points on the western waterways. "Elder Brother," said a Chippewa chief in the course of one of the interminable harangues delivered during the negotiation, "you asked who were the true owners of the land now ceded to the United States. In answer, I tell you, if any nations should call themselves the owners of it, they would be guilty of falsehood; our claim to it is equal; our Elder Brother has conquered it." The United States duly recognized the Indian title to all lands not expressly ceded and promised the Indians annual subsidies. The terms of the treaty were faithfully observed on both sides, and for fifteen years the pioneer lived and toiled in peace.

Wayne forthwith became a national hero. Returning to Philadelphia in 1796, he was met by a guard of honor, hailed with the ringing of bells and a salute of fifteen guns, and treated to a dazzling display of fireworks. Congress voted its thanks, and Washington, whose fears had long since vanished, added his congratulations. There was one other service on the frontier for the doughty general to render. The British posts were at last to be surrendered, and Wayne was designated to receive them. By midsummer he was back in the forest country, and in the autumn he took possession of Detroit, amid acclamations of Indians, Americans, Frenchmen, and Englishmen alike. But his work was done. On the return journey he suffered a renewed attack of his old enemy, gout, and at Presqu'isle (Erie) he died. A blockhouse modeled on the defenses which he built during his western campaign marks his first resting-place and bears aloft the flag which he helped plant in the heart of the Continent.

Chapter VI.

The Great Migration

While the fate of the Northwest still hung in the balance, emigration from the eastern States became the rage. "Every small farmer whose barren acres were covered with mortgages, whose debts pressed heavily upon him, or whose roving spirit gave him no peace, was eager to sell his homestead for what it would bring and begin life anew on the banks of the Muskingum or the Ohio."* Land companies were then just as optimistic and persuasive as they are today, and the attractions of the western country lost nothing in the telling. Pamphlets described the climate as luxurious, the soil as inexhaustible, the rainfall as both abundant and well distributed, the crops as unfailingly bountiful; paid agents went among the people assuring them that a man of push and courage could nowhere be so prosperous and so happy as in the West.

* McMaster, "History of the People of the United States," vol. III, p. 461.

As early as 1787 an observer at Pittsburgh reported that in six weeks he saw fifty flatboats set off for the downriver settlements; in 1788 forty-five hundred emigrants were said to have passed Fort Harmar between February and June. Most of these people were bound for Kentucky or Tennessee. But the census of 1790 gave the population north of the Ohio as 4,280, and after Wayne's victory the proportion of newcomers who fixed their abodes in that part of the country rapidly increased. For a decade Ohio was the favorite goal; and within eight years after the battle at Fallen Timbers this region was ready for admission to the Union as a State. Southern Indiana also filled rapidly.

For a time the westward movement was regarded as of no disadvantage to the seaboard States. It was supposed that the frontier would attract a population of such character as could easily be spared in more settled communities. But it became apparent that the new country did not appeal simply to broken-down farmers, bankrupts, and ne'er-do-wells. Robust and industrious men, with growing families, were drawn off in great numbers; and public protest was raised against the "plots to drain the East of its best blood." Anti-emigration pamphlets were scattered broadcast, and, after the manner of the day, the leading western enterprises were belabored with much bad verse. A rude cut which gained wide circulation represented a stout, ruddy, well-dressed man on a sleek horse, with a label, "I am going to Ohio," meeting a pale and ghastly skeleton of a man, in rags, on the wreck of what had once been a horse, with the label, "I have been to Ohio."

The streams of migration flowed from many sources. New England contributed heavily. Marietta, Cincinnati, and many other rising river towns received some of the best blood of that remote section. The Western Reserve - a tract bordering on Lake Erie which Connecticut had not ceded to the Federal Government - drew largely from the Nutmeg State. A month before

Wayne set out to take possession of Detroit, Moses Cleaveland with a party of fifty Connecticut homeseekers started off to found a settlement in the Reserve; and the town which took its name from the leader was but the first of a score which promptly sprang up in this inviting district. The "Seven Ranges," lying directly south of the Reserve, drew emigrants from Pennsylvania, with some from farther south. The Scioto valley attracted chiefly Virginians, who early made Chillicothe their principal center. In the west, and north of the Symmes tract, Kentuckians poured in by the thousands.

Thus in a decade Ohio became a frontier melting-pot. Puritan, Cavalier, Irishman, Scotch-Irishman, German - all were poured into the crucible. Ideals clashed, and differing customs grated harshly. But the product of a hundred years of cross-breeding was a splendid type of citizenship. At the presidential inaugural ceremonies of March 4, 1881, six men chiefly attracted the attention of the crowd: the retiring President, Hayes; the incoming President, Garfield; the Chief-Justice who administered the oath, Waite; the general commanding the army, William T. Sherman; the ex-Secretary of the Treasury, John Sherman; and "the Marshal Ney of America," Lieutenant-General Sheridan. Five of the six were natives of Ohio, and the sixth was a lifelong resident. Men commented on the striking group and rightly remarked that it could have been produced only by a singularly happy blending of the ideas and ideals that form the warp and woof of Americanism.

Amalgamation, however, took time; for there were towering prejudices and antipathies to be overcome. The Yankee scorned the Southerner, who reciprocated with a double measure of dislike. The New England settlers were, as a rule, people of some education; not one of their communities long went without a schoolmaster. They were pious, law-abiding, industrious; their more easygoing neighbors were likely to consider them over-sensitive and critical. But the quality that made most impression upon others was their shrewdness in business transactions. They could drive a bargain and could discover loopholes in a contract in a fashion to take the average backwoodsman off his feet. "Yankee tricks" became, indeed, a household phrase wherever New Englander and Southerner met. Whether the Yankee talked or kept silent, whether he was generous or parsimonious, he was always under suspicion.

What of the "Long Knives" from Virginia, the Carolinas, and Kentucky who also made the Ohio lands their goal? Of books they knew little; they did not name their settlements in honor of classic heroes. They were not "gentlemen"; many of them, indeed, had sought the West to escape a society in which distinctions of birth and possessions had put them at a disadvantage. They were not so pious as the New Englanders, though they were capable of great religious enthusiasm, and their morals were probably not inferior. Their houses were poorer; their villages were not so well kept; their dress was more uncouth, and their ways rougher. But they were a hardy folk - brave, industrious, hospitable, and generous to a fault.

In the first days of westward migration the favorite gateway into the Ohio Valley was Cumberland Gap, at the southeastern corner of the present State of Kentucky. Thence the Virginians and Carolinians passed easily to the Ohio in the region of Cincinnati or Louisville. Later emigrants from more northern States found other serviceable routes. Until the opening of the Erie Canal in 1825, New Englanders reached the West by three main avenues. Some followed the Mohawk and Genesee turnpikes across central New York to Lake Erie. This route led directly, of course, to the Western Reserve. Some traveled along the Catskill turnpike from the Hudson to the headwaters of the Allegheny, and thence descended the Ohio. Still others went by boat from Boston to New York, Philadelphia, or Baltimore, in order to approach the Ohio by a more southerly course.

The natural outlet from Pennsylvania was the Ohio River. Emigrants from the western parts of the State floated down the Allegheny or Monongahela to the main stream. Those from farther east, including settlers from New Jersey, made the journey overland by one of several well-known roads. The best of these was a turnpike following the line that General Forbes had cut during the French and Indian War from Philadelphia to Pittsburgh by way of Lancaster and Bedford. Baltimore was a favorite point of departure, and from it the route lay almost invariably along a turnpike to Cumberland on the upper Potomac, and thence by the National Road across the mountains to Wheeling. In later days this was the route chiefly taken from Virginia, although more southerly passes through the Blue Ridge were used as outlets to the Great Kanawha, the Big Sandy, and other streams flowing into the Ohio farther down.

Thus the lines of westward travel which in the East spread fan-shape from Maine to Georgia converged on the Ohio; and that stream became, and for half a century remained, the great pathway of empire. Most of the emigrants had to cover long distances in overland travel before they reached the hospitable waterway; some, especially in earlier times, made the entire journey by land. Hundreds of the very poor went afoot, carrying all their earthly possessions on their backs, or dragging them in rude carts. But the usual conveyance was the canvas-covered wagon - ancestor of the "prairie schooner" of the western plains - drawn over the rough and muddy roads by four, or even six, horses. In this vehicle the emigrants stowed their provisions, household furniture and utensils, agricultural implements, looms, seeds, medicines, and every sort of thing that the prudent householder expected to need, and for which he could find space. Extra horses or oxen sometimes drew an additional load; cattle, and even flocks of sheep, were occasionally driven ahead or behind by some member of the family.

In the years of heaviest migration the highways converging on Pittsburgh and Wheeling were fairly crowded with westward-flowing traffic. As a rule several families, perhaps from the same neighborhood in the old home, traveled together; and in any case the chance acquaintances of the road and of the wayside inns broke the loneliness of the journey. There were wonderful things to be seen, and every day brought novel experiences. But exposure and illness, dread of Indian attacks, mishaps of every sort, and the awful sense of isolation and of uncertainty of the future, caused many a man's stout heart to quail, and brought anguish unspeakable to brave women. Of such joys and sorrows, however, is a frontier existence compounded; and of the growing thousands who turned their faces toward the setting sun, comparatively few yielded to discouragement and went back East. Those who did so were usually the land speculators and people of weak, irresolute, or shiftless character.

An English traveler, Morris Birkbeck, who passed over the National Road through southwestern Pennsylvania in 1817, was filled with amazement at the number, hardihood, and determination of the emigrants whom he encountered.

"Old America seems to be breaking up [he wrote] and moving westward. We are seldom out of sight, as we travel on this grand track, towards the Ohio, of family groups, behind and before us.... A small wagon (so light that you might almost carry it, yet strong enough to bear a good load of bedding, utensils and provisions, and a swarm of young citizens - and to sustain marvelous shocks in its passage over these rocky heights) with two small horses; sometimes a cow or two, comprises their all; excepting a little store of hard-earned cash for the land office of the district; where they may obtain a title for as many acres as they possess half-dollars, being one fourth of the purchase money. The wagon has a tilt, or cover, made of a sheet, or perhaps a blanket. The family are seen before, behind, or within the vehicle, according to the road or the weather, or perhaps the spirits of the party.... A cart and single horse frequently affords the means of transfer, sometimes a horse and pack-saddle. Often the back of the poor pilgrim bears all his effects, and his wife follows, naked-footed, bending under the hopes of the family."*

* Quoted in Turner, "Rise of the New West," pp. 79-80.

Arrived at the Ohio, the emigrant either engaged passage on some form of river-craft or set to work to construct with his own hands a vessel that would bear him and his belongings to the promised land. The styles of river-craft that appeared on the Ohio and other western streams in the great era of river migration make a remarkable pageant. There were canoes, pirogues, skiffs, rafts, dugouts, scows, galleys, arks, keelboats, flatboats, barges, "broadhorns," "sneak-boxes," and eventually ocean-going brigs, schooners, and steamboats. The canoe served the early explorer and trader, and even the settler whose possessions had been carried over the Alleghanies on a single packhorse. But after the Revolution the needs of an awakening empire led to the introduction of new types of craft, built to afford a maximum of capacity and safety on a downward voyage, without regard for the demands of a round trip. The most common of these one-way vessels was the flatboat.

A flatboat trip down the great river was likely to be filled with excitement. The sound of the steam-dredge had never been heard on the western waters, and the streambed was as Nature had made it, or rather was continually remaking it. Yearly floods washed out new channels and formed new reefs and sand-bars, while logs and brush borne from the heavily forested banks continually built new obstructions. Consequently the sharpest lookout had to be maintained, and the pilot was both skilful and lucky who completed his trip without permitting his boat to be caught on a "planter" (a log immovably fixed in the river bed), entangled in the branches of overhanging trees, driven on an island, or dashed on the bank at a bend. Navigation by night and on foggy days was hazardous in the extreme and was avoided as far as possible. If all went well, the voyage from Pittsburgh to Cincinnati could be completed in six or eight days; but delays might easily extend the period to a month.

One grave danger has not been mentioned - the Indians. From the moment when the slow-moving flatboat passed beyond the protection of a white settlement, it was liable to be fired on, by day or by night, by redskins; and the better-built boats were so constructed as to be at least partially bullet-proof. Sometimes extra timber was used to give safety; sometimes the cargo was specially placed with that aim in view. The Indians rarely went beyond the water's edge. Their favorite ruse was to cause captive or renegade whites to run along the bank imploring to be saved. When a boat had been decoyed to shore, and perhaps a landing had been made, the savages would pour a murderous fire on the voyagers. This practice became so common that pioneer boats "shunned the whites who hailed them from the shores as they would have shunned the Indians," and as a consequence many whites escaping from the Indians in the interior were refused succor and left to die.

When the flatboat reached its destination, it might find service as a floating store, or even as a schoolhouse. But it was likely to be broken up, so that the materials in it could be used for building purposes. Before sawmills became common, lumber was a precious commodity, and hundreds of pioneer cabins in the Ohio Valley were built partly or wholly of the boards and timbers taken from the flatboats of their owners. Even the "gunnels" were sometimes used in Cincinnati as foundations for houses. In later days the flatboat, if in reasonably good condition, was not unlikely to be sold to persons engaged in trading down the Mississippi. Loaded with grain, flour, meats, and other backwoods products, it would descend to Natchez or

New Orleans, where its cargo could be transferred to ocean-going craft. But in any case its end was the same; for it would not have been profitable, even had it been physically possible, to move the heavy, ungainly craft upstream over long distances, in order to keep it continuously in service.

Chapter VII.

Pioneer Days And Ways

Arrived on the lower Ohio, or one of its tributaries, the pioneer looked out upon a land of remarkable riches. It was not a Mexico or a Peru, with emblazoned palaces and glittering temples, nor yet a California, with gold-flecked sands. It was merely an unending stretch of wooded hills and grassy plains, bedecked with majestic forests and fructifying rivers and lakes. It had no treasures save for the man of courage, industry, and patience; but for such it held home, broad acres, liberty, and the coveted opportunity for social equality and advancement.

The new country has been commonly thought of, and referred to by writers on the history of the West, as a "wilderness"; and offhand, one might suppose that the settlers were obliged literally to hew their way through densely grown vegetation to the spots which they selected for their homes. In point of fact, there were great areas of upland - not alone in the prairie country of northern Indiana and Illinois, but in the hilly regions within a hundred miles of the Ohio - that were almost treeless. On these unobstructed stretches grasses grew in profusion; and here roamed great herds of herbivorous animal-kind - deer and elk, and also buffalo, "filing in grave procession to drink at the rivers, plunging and snorting among the rapids and quicksands, rolling their huge bulk on the grass, rushing upon each other in hot encounter, like champions under shield." Along the watercourses ducks, wild geese, cranes, herons, and other fowl sounded their harsh cries; gray squirrels, prairie chickens, and partridges the hunter found at every turn.

Furthermore, the forests, as a rule, were not difficult to penetrate. The trees stood thick, but deer paths, buffalo roads, and Indian trails ramified in all directions, and sometimes were wide enough to allow two or three wagons to advance abreast. Mighty poplars, beeches, sycamores, and "sugars" pushed to great heights in quest of air and sunshine, and often their intertwining branches were locked solidly together by a heavy growth of grape or other vines, producing a canopy which during the summer months permitted scarcely a ray of sunlight to reach the ground. There was, therefore, a notable absence of undergrowth. When a tree died and decayed, it fell apart piecemeal; it was with difficulty that woodsmen could wrest a giant oak or poplar from its moorings and bring it to the ground, even by severing the trunk completely at the base. Here and there a clean swath was cut through a forest, for perhaps dozens of miles, by a hurricane. This gave opportunity for the growth of a thicket of bushes and small trees, and such spots were equally likely to be the habitations of wild beasts and the hiding-places of warlike bands of redskins.

There were always adventurous pioneers who scorned the settlements and went off with their families to fix their abodes in isolated places. But the average newcomer preferred to find a location in, or reasonably near, a settlement. The choice of a site, whether by a company of immigrants wishing to establish a settlement or by an individual settler, was a matter of much importance. Some thought must be given to facilities for fortification against hostile natives. There must be an adequate supply of drinking-water; and the location of innumerable pioneer dwellings was selected with reference to free-flowing springs. Pasture land for immediate use was desirable; and of course the soil must be fertile. As a rule, the settler had the alternative of establishing himself on the lowlands along a stream and obtaining ground of the greatest productiveness, with the almost certain prospect of annual attacks of malaria, or of seeking the poorer but more healthful uplands. The attractions of the "bottoms" were frequently irresistible, and the "ague" became a feature of frontier life almost as inevitable as the proverbial "death and taxes."

The site selected, the next task was to clear a few acres of ground where the cabin was to stand. It was highly desirable to have a belt of open land as a protection against Indians and wild beasts; besides, there must be fields cleared for tillage. If the settler had neighbors, he was likely to have their aid in cutting away the densest growth of trees, and in raising into position the heavy timbers which formed the framework and walls of his cabin. Splendid oaks, poplars, and sycamores were cut into convenient lengths, and such as could not be used were rolled into great heaps and burned. Before sawmills were introduced lumber could not be manufactured; afterwards, it became so plentiful as to have small market value.

Almost without exception the frontier cabins had log walls; and they were rarely of larger size than single lengths would permit. On an average, they were twelve or fourteen feet wide and fifteen or eighteen feet long. Sometimes they were divided into two rooms, with an attic above; frequently there was but one room "downstairs." The logs were notched together at the corners, and the spaces between them were filled with moss or clay or covered with bark. Rafters were affixed to the uppermost logs, and to one another, with wooden pins driven through auger holes. In earliest times the roof was of bark; later on, shingles were used, although nails were long unknown, and the shingles, after being laid in rows, were weighted down with straight logs.

Sometimes there was only an earth floor. But as a rule "puncheons," i.e., thick, rough boards split from logs, were laid crosswise on round logs and were fastened with wooden pins. There was commonly but a single door, which was made also of puncheons and hung on wooden hinges. A favorite device was to construct the door in upper and lower sections, so as to make it possible, when there came a knock or a call from the outside, to respond without offering easy entrance to an unwelcome visitor. In the days when there was considerable danger of Indian attacks no windows were constructed, for the householder could defend only one aperture. Later, square holes which could be securely barred at night and during cold weather were made to serve as windows. Flat pieces of sandstone, if they could be found, were used in building the great fireplace; otherwise, thick timbers heavily covered with clay were made to serve. In scarcely a cabin was there a trace of iron or glass; the whole could be constructed with only two implements - an ax and an auger.

Occasionally a family carried to its new home some

treasured bits of furniture; but the difficulty of transportation was likely to be prohibitive, and as a rule the cabins contained only such pieces of furniture as could be fashioned on the spot. A table was made by mounting a smoothed slab on four posts, set in auger holes. For seats short benches and three-legged stools, constructed after the manner of the tables, were in common use. Cooking utensils, food-supplies, seeds, herbs for medicinal purposes, and all sorts of household appliances were stowed away on shelves, made by laying clapboards across wooden pins driven into the wall and mounting to the ceiling; although after sawed lumber came into use it was a matter of no great difficulty to construct chests and cupboards. Not infrequently the settler's family slept on bear skins or blankets stretched on the floor. But crude bedsteads were made by erecting a pole with a fork in such a manner that other poles could be supported horizontally in this fork and by crevices in the walls. Split boards served as "slats" on which the bedding was spread. For a long time "straw-ticks" - large cloth bags filled with straw or sometimes dry grass or leaves - were articles of luxury. Iron pots and knives were necessities which the wise householder carried with him from his eastern or southern home. In the West they were hard to obtain. The chief source of supply was the iron-manufacturing districts of Pennsylvania and Virginia, whence the wares were carried to the entrepots of river trade by packhorses. The kitchen outfit of the average newcomer was completed with a few pewter dishes, plates, and spoons. But winter evenings were utilized in whittling out wooden bowls, trenchers, and noggins or cups, while gourds and hard-shelled squashes were turned to numerous uses. The commonest drinking utensil was a long-handled gourd.

The dress of the pioneer long remained a curious cross between that of the Indians and that of the white people of the older sections. In earlier times the hunting-shirt - made of linsey, coarse nettle-bark linen, buffalo-hair, or even dressed deerskins - was universally worn by the men, together with breeches, leggings, and moccasins. The women and children were dressed in simple garments of linsey. In warm weather they went barefooted; in cold, they wore moccasins or coarse shoes.

Rarely was there lack of food for these pioneer families. The soil was prodigal, and the forests abounded in game. The piece de resistance of the backwoods menu was "hog an' hominy"; that is to say, pork served with Indian corn which, after being boiled in lye to remove the hulls, had been soaked in clear water and cooked soft. "Johnny cake" and "pone" - two varieties of cornbread - were regularly eaten at breakfast and dinner. The standard dish for supper was cornmeal mush and milk. As cattle were not numerous, the housewife often lacked milk, in which case she fell back on her one never-failing resource - hominy; or she served the mush with sweetened water, molasses, the gravy of fried meat, or even bear's oil. Tea and coffee were long unknown, and when introduced they were likely to be scorned by the men as "slops" good enough perhaps for women and children. Vegetables the settlers grew in the garden plot which ordinarily adjoined the house, and thrifty families had also a "truck patch" in which they raised pumpkins, squashes, potatoes, beans, melons, and corn for "roasting ears." The forests yielded game, as well as fruits and wild grapes, and honey for sweetening.

The first quality for which the life of the frontier called

was untiring industry. It was possible, of course, to eke out an existence by hunting, fishing, petty trading, and garnering the fruits which Nature supplied without man's assistance. And many pioneers in whom the roving instinct was strong went on from year to year in this hand-to-mouth fashion. But the settler who expected to be a real home-builder, to gain some measure of wealth, to give his children a larger opportunity in life, must be prepared to work, to plan, to economize, and to sacrifice. The forests had to be felled; the great logs had to be rolled together and burned; crops of maize, tobacco, oats, and cane needed to be planted, cultivated, and harvested; live-stock to be housed and fed; fences and barns to be built; pork, beef, grain, whiskey, and other products to be prepared for market, and perhaps carried scores of miles to a place of shipment.

All these things had to be done under conditions of exceptional difficulty. The settler never knew what night his place would be raided by marauding redskins, who would be lenient indeed if they merely carried off part of his cattle or burned his barn. Any morning he might peer out of the "port hole" above the cabin door to see skulking figures awaiting their chance. Sickness, too, was a menace and a terror. Picture the horrors of isolation in times of emergency - wife or child suddenly taken desperately ill, and no physician within a hundred miles; husband or son hovering between life and death as the result of injury by a falling tree, a wild beast, a venomous snake, an accidental gun-shot, or the tomahawk of a prowling Indian. Who shall describe the anxiety, the agony, which in some measure must have been the lot of every frontier family? The prosaic illnesses of the flesh were troublesome enough. On account of defective protection for the feet in wet weather, almost everybody had rheumatism; most settlers in the bottom-lands fell victims to fever and ague at one time or another; even in the hill country few persons wholly escaped malarial disorders. "When this home-building and land-clearing is accomplished," wrote one whose recollections of the frontier were vivid, "a faithful picture would reveal not only the changes that have been wrought, but a host of prematurely brokedown men and women, besides an undue proportion resting peacefully in country graveyards."

The frontiersman's best friend was his trusty rifle. With it he defended his cabin and his crops from marauders, waged warfare on hostile redskins, and obtained the game which formed an indispensable part of his food supply. At first the gun chiefly used on the border was the smooth-bored musket. But toward the close of the eighteenth century a gunsmith named Deckhard, living at Lancaster, Pennsylvania, began making flintlock rifles of small bore, and in a short time the "Deckhard rifle" was to be found in the hands of almost every backwoodsman. The barrel was heavy and from three feet to three feet and a half in length, so that the piece, when set on the ground, reached at least to the huntsman's shoulder. The bore was cut with twisting grooves, and was so small that seventy bullets were required to weigh a pound. In loading, a greased linen "patch" was wrapped around the bullet; and only a small charge of powder was needed. The grin was heavy to carry and difficult to hold steadily upon a target; but it was economical of ammunition, and in the hands of the strong-muscled, keen-eyed, iron-nerved frontiersman it was an exceedingly accurate weapon, at all events within the ordinary limits of forest ranges. He was a poor marksman who could not shoot running deer or elk at a distance of one hundred and fifty yards, and kill ducks and geese on the wing; and "boys of twelve hung their heads in shame if detected in hitting a squirrel in any other part of the body than its head."

Life on the frontier was filled with hard work, danger, and anxiety. Yet it had its lighter side, and, indeed, it may be doubted whether people anywhere relished sport more keenly or found more pleasure in their everyday pursuits. The occasional family without neighbors was likely to suffer from loneliness. But few of the settlers were thus cut off, and as a rule community life was not only physically possible but highly developed. Many were the opportunities that served to bring together the frontiersmen, with their families, throughout a settlement or county. Foremost among such occasions were the log-rollings.

After a settler had felled the thick-growing trees on a plot which he desired to prepare for cultivation, he cut them, either by sawing or by burning, into logs twelve or fifteen feet in length. Frequently these were three, four, or even five feet in diameter, so that they could not be moved by one man, even with a team of horses. In such a situation, the settler would send word to his neighbors for miles around that on a given day there would be a log-rolling at his place; and when the day arrived six, or a dozen, or perhaps a score, of sturdy men, with teams of horses and yokes of oxen, and very likely accompanied by members of their families, would arrive on the scene with merry shouts of anticipation. By means of handspikes and chains drawn by horses or oxen, the great timbers were pushed, rolled, and dragged into heaps, and by nightfall the field lay open and ready for the plough - requiring, at the most, only the burning of the huge piles that had been gathered.

Without loss of time the fires were started; and as darkness came on, the countryside glowed as with the light of a hundred huge torches. The skies were reddened, and as a mighty oak or poplar log toppled and fell to the ground, showers of sparks lent the scene volcanic splendor. Bats and owls and other dim-eyed creatures of the night flew about in bewilderment, sometimes bumping hard against fences or other objects, sometimes plunging madly into the flames and contributing to the general holocaust. For days the great fires were kept going, until the last remnants of this section of the once imposing forest were consumed; while smoke hung far out over the country, producing an atmospheric effect like that of Indian summer.

Heavy exertion called for generous refreshment, and on these occasions the host could be depended on to provide an abundance of food and drink. The little cabin could hardly be made to accommodate so many guests, even in relays. Accordingly, a long table was constructed with planks and trestles in a shady spot, and at noon - and perhaps again in the evening - the women folk served a meal which at least made up in "staying qualities" what it lacked in variety or delicacy. The principal dish was almost certain to be "pot-pie," consisting of boiled turkeys, geese, chickens, grouse, veal, or venison, with an abundance of dumplings. This, with cornbread and milk, met the demands of the occasion; but if the host was able to furnish a cask of rum, his generosity was thoroughly appreciated.

In the autumn, corn-huskings were a favorite form of diversion, especially for the young people; and in the early spring neighbors sometimes came together to make maple sugar. A wedding was an important event and furnished diversion of a different kind. From distances of twenty and thirty miles people came to attend the ceremony, and often the festivities extended over two or three days. Even now there was work to be done; for as a rule the neighbors organized a house-building "bee," and before separating for their homes they constructed a cabin for the newly wedded pair, or at all events brought it sufficiently near completion to be finished by the young husband himself.

Even after a day of heavy toil at log-rolling, the young men and boys bantered one another into foot races, wrestling matches, shooting contests, and other feats of strength or skill. And if a fiddler could be found, the day was sure to end with a "hoe-down" - a dance that "made even the log-walled house tremble." No corn-husking or wedding was complete without dancing, although members of certain of the more straitlaced religious sects already frowned upon the diversion.

Rough conditions of living made rough men, and we need not be surprised by the testimony of English and American travelers, that the frontier had more than its share of boisterous fun, rowdyism, lawlessness, and crime. The taste for whiskey was universal, and large quantities were manufactured in rude stills, not only for shipment down the Mississippi, but for local consumption. Frequenters of the river-town taverns called for their favorite brands - "Race Horse," "Moral Suasion," "Vox Populi," "Pig and Whistle," or "Split Ticket," as the case might be. But the average frontiersman cared little for the niceties of color or flavor so long as his liquor was cheap and produced the desired effect. Hard work and a monotonous diet made him continually thirsty; and while ordinarily he drank only water and milk at home, at the taverns and at social gatherings he often succumbed to potations which left him in happy drunken forgetfulness of daily hardships. House-raisings and weddings often became orgies marked by quarreling and fighting and terminating in brutal and bloody brawls. Foreign visitors to the back country were led to comment frequently on the number of men who had lost an eye or an ear, or had been otherwise maimed in these rough-and-tumble contests.

The great majority of the frontiersmen, however, were sober, industrious, and law-abiding folk; and they were by no means beyond the pale of religion. On account of the numbers of Scotch-Irish, Presbyterianism was in earlier days the principal creed. although there were many Catholics and adherents of the Reformed Dutch and German churches, and even a few Episcopalians. About the beginning of the nineteenth century sectarian ascendancy passed to the Methodists and Baptists, whose ranks were rapidly recruited by means of one of the most curious and characteristic of backwoods institutions, the camp-meeting "revival." The years 1799 and 1800 brought the first of the several great waves of religious excitement by which the West - especially Ohio, Indiana, Kentucky, and Tennessee was periodically swept until within the memory of men still living.

Camp-meetings were usually planned and managed by Methodist circuit-riders or Baptist itinerant preachers, who hesitated not to carry their work into the remotest and most dangerous parts of the back country. When the news went abroad that such a meeting was to take place, people flocked to the scene from far and near, in wagons, on horseback, and on foot. Pious men and women came for the sake of religious fellowship and inspiration; others not so pious came from motives of curiosity, or even to share in the rough sport for which the scoffers always found opportunity. The meeting lasted days, and even weeks; and preaching, praying, singing, "testifying," and "exhorting" went on almost without intermission. "The preachers became frantic in their exhortations; men, women, and children, falling as if in catalepsy, were laid out in rows. Shouts, incoherent singing, sometimes barking as of an unreasoning beast, rent the air. Convulsive leaps and dancing were common; so, too, 'jerking,' stakes being driven into the ground to jerk by, the subjects of the fit grasping them as they writhed and grimaced in their contortions. The world, indeed, seemed demented."* Whole communities sometimes professed conversion; and it was considered a particularly good day's work when notorious disbelievers or wrong-doers - "hard bats," in the phraseology of the frontier - or gangs of young rowdies whose only object in coming was to commit acts of deviltry, succumbed to the peculiarly compelling influences of the occasion.

* Hosmer, "Short History of the Mississippi Valley," p. 116.

In this sort of religion there was, of course, much wild emotionalism and sheer hysteria; and there were always people to whom it was repellent. Backsliders were numerous, and the person who "fell from grace" was more than likely to revert to his earlier wickedness in its grossest forms. None the less, in a rough, unlearned, and materialistic society such spiritual shakings-up were bound to yield much permanent good. Most western people, at one time or another, came under the influence of the Methodist and Baptist revivals; and from the men and women who were drawn by them to a new and larger view of life were recruited the hundreds of little congregations whose meeting-houses in the course of time dotted the hills and plains from the Alleghanies to the Mississippi. As for the hard-working, honest-minded frontier preachers who braved every sort of danger in the performance of their great task, the West owes them an eternal debt of gratitude. In the words of Roosevelt, "their prejudices and narrow dislikes, their raw vanity and sullen distrust of all who were better schooled than they, count for little when weighed against their intense earnestness and heroic self-sacrifice."

Nor was education neglected. Many of the settlers, especially those who came from the South, were illiterate. But all who made any pretense of respectability were desirous of giving their children an opportunity to learn to read and write. Accordingly, wherever half a dozen families lived reasonably close together, a log schoolhouse was sure to be found. In the days before public funds existed for the support of education the teachers were paid directly, and usually in produce, by the patrons. Sometimes a wandering pedagogue would find his way into a community and, being engaged to give instruction for two or three months during the winter, would "board around" among the residents and take such additional pay as he could get. More often, some one of the settlers who was fortunate enough to possess the rudiments of an education undertook the role of schoolmaster in the interval between the autumn corn-gathering and the spring ploughing and planting.

Instruction rarely extended beyond the three R's; but occasionally a newcomer who had somewhere picked up a smattering of algebra, Latin, or astronomy stirred the wonder, if not also the suspicion, of the neighborhood. Schoolbooks were few and costly; crude slates were made from pieces of shale; pencils were fashioned from varicolored soapstone found in the beds of small streams. No frontier picture is more familiar or more pleasing than that of the farmer's boy sitting or lying on the floor during the long winter evening industriously tracing by firelight or by candlelight the proverb or quotation assigned him as an exercise in penmanship, or wrestling with the intricacies of least common denominators and highest common divisors. It is in such a setting that we get our first glimpse of the greatest of western Americans, Abraham Lincoln.

Chapter VIII.

Tecumseh

Wayne's victory in 1795, followed by the Treaty of Fort Greenville, gave the Northwest welcome relief from Indian warfare, and within four years the Territory was ready to be advanced to the second of the three grades of government provided for it in the Ordinance of 1787. A Legislature was set up at Cincinnati, and in due time it proceeded to the election of a delegate to Congress. Choice fell on a young man whose name was destined to a permanent place in the country's history. William Henry Harrison was the son of a signer of the Declaration of Independence, the scion of one of Virginia's most honored families. Entering the army in 1791, he had served as an aide-de-camp to Wayne in the campaign which ended at Fallen Timbers, and at the time of his election was acting as Secretary of the Territory and ex-officio Lieutenant-Governor.

Although but twenty-six years of age, and without a vote in the House of Representatives, Harrison succeeded in procuring from Congress in 1800 an act dividing the Territory into two distinct "governments," separated by the old Greenville treaty line as far as Fort Recovery and then by a line running due north to the Canadian boundary. The division to the east was named Ohio, that to the west Indiana; and Harrison was made Governor of the latter, with his residence at Vincennes. In 1802 the development of the back country was freshly emphasized by the admission of Ohio as a State.

Meanwhile the equilibrium between the white man and the red again became unstable. In the Treaty of 1795 the natives had ceded only southern Ohio, southeastern Indiana, and a few other small and scattered areas. Northward and westward, their country stretched to the Lakes and the Mississippi, unbroken except by military posts and widely scattered settlements; and title to all of this territory had been solemnly guaranteed. As late as 1800 the white population of what is now Indiana was practically confined to Clark's Grant, near the falls of the Ohio, and a small region around Vincennes. It numbered not more than twenty-five hundred persons. But thereafter immigration from the seaboard States, and from the nearer lands of Kentucky and Tennessee, set in on a new scale. By 1810 Indiana had a white population of twenty-five thousand, and the cabins of the energetic settlers dotted river valleys and hillsides never before trodden by white man.

In this new rush of pioneers the rights of the Indians received scant consideration. Hardy and well-armed Virginians and Kentuckians broke across treaty boundaries and possessed themselves of fertile lands to which they had no valid claim. White hunters trespassed far and wide on Indian territory, until by 1810 great regions, which a quarter of a century earlier abounded in deer, bear, and buffalo, were made as useless for Indian purposes as barren wastes. Although entitled to the protection of law in his person and property, the native was cheated and overawed at every turn; he might even be murdered with impunity. Abraham Lincoln's uncle thought it a virtuous act to shoot an Indian on sight, and the majority of pioneers agreed with him.

"I can tell at once," wrote Harrison in 1801, "upon looking at an Indian whom I may chance to meet whether he belongs to a neighboring or a more distant tribe. The latter is generally well-clothed, healthy, and vigorous; the former half-naked, filthy, and enfeebled by intoxication, and many of them without arms excepting a knife, which they carry for the most villainous purposes." The stronger tribes perceived quite as clearly as did the Governor the ruinous effects of contact between the two peoples, and the steady destruction of the border warriors became a leading cause of discontent. Congress had passed laws intended to prevent the sale of spiritucus liquors to the natives, but the courts had construed these measures to be operative only outside the bounds of States and organized Territories, and in the great unorganized Northwest the laws were not heeded, and the ruinous traffic went on uninterrupted. Harrison reported that when there were only six hundred warriors on the Wabash the annual consumption of whiskey there was six thousand gallons, and that killing each other in drunken brawls had "become so customary that it was no longer thought criminal."

Most exasperating, however, from the red man's point of view was the insatiable demand of the newcomers for land. In the years 1803, 1804, and 1805 Harrison made treaties with the remnants of the Miami, Eel River, Piankeshaw, and Delaware tribes - characterized by him as "a body of the most depraved wretches on earth" - which gained for the settlers a strip of territory fifty miles wide south of White River; and in 1809 he similarly acquired, by the Treaty of Fort Wayne, three million acres, in tracts which cut into the heart of the Indian country for almost a hundred miles up both banks of the Wabash. The Wabash valley was richer in game than any other region south of Lake Michigan, and its loss was keenly felt by the Indians. Indeed, it was mainly the cession of 1809 that brought once more to a crisis the long-brewing difficulties with the Indians.

About the year 1768 the Creek squaw of a Shawnee warrior gave birth at one time to three boys, in the vicinity of the present city of Springfield, Ohio.* One of the three barely left his name in aboriginal annals. A second, known as Laulewasikaw, "the man with the loud voice," poses in the pages of history as "the prophet." The third brother was Tecumseh, "the wild-cat that leaps upon its prey," or "the shooting star," as the name has been translated. He is described as a tall, handsome warrior - daring and energetic, of fluent and persuasive speech, given to deep reflection, an implacable hater of the white man. Other qualities he possessed which were not so common among his people. He had perfect self-command, a keen insight into human motives and purposes, and an exceptional capacity to frame plans and organize men to carry them out. His crowning scheme for bringing together the tribes of the Middle West into a grand democratic confederacy to regulate land cessions and other dealings with the whites stamps him as perhaps the most statesmanlike member of his race.

* Authorities differ as to the facts of Tecumseh's birth. His earliest biographer, Benjamin Drake, holds that he was "wholly a Shawanoe" and that he was a fourth

child, the Prophet and another son being twins. William Henry Harrison spoke of Tecumseh's mother as a Creek.

While yet hardly more than a boy, Tecumseh seems to have been stirred to deep indignation by the persistent encroachment of the whites upon the hunting-grounds of his fathers. The cessions of 1804 and 1805 he specially resented, and it is not unlikely that they clinched the decision of the young warrior to take up the task which Pontiac had left unfinished. At all events, the plan was soon well in hand. A less far-seeing leader would have been content to call the scattered tribes to a momentary alliance with a view to a general uprising against the invaders. But Tecumseh's purposes ran far deeper. All of the Indian peoples, of whatever name or relationships, from the Lakes to the Gulf and from the Alleghanies to the Rockies, were to be organized in a single, permanent confederacy. This union, furthermore, was to consist, not of chieftains, but of the warriors; and its governing body was to be a warriors' congress, an organ of genuine popular rule. Joint ownership of all Indian lands was to be assumed by the confederacy, and the piecemeal cession of territory by petty tribal chiefs, under pressure of government agents, was to be made impossible. Only thus, Tecumseh argued, could the red man hope to hold his own in the uneven contest that was going on.

The plan was brilliant, even though impracticable. Naturally, it did not appeal instantly to the chieftains, for it took away - tribal independence and undermined the chieftain's authority. Besides, its author was not a chief, and had no sanction of birth or office. Its success was dependent on the building of an intertribal association such as Indian history had never known. And while there was nothing in it which contravened the professed policy of the United States, it ran counter to the irrepressible tendency of the advancing white population to spread at will over the great western domain.

By these obstacles Tecumseh was not deterred. With indefatigable zeal he traveled from one end of the country to the other, arguing with chiefs, making fervid speeches to assembled warriors, and in every possible manner impressing his people with his great idea. The Prophet went with him; and when the orator's logic failed to carry, conviction, the medicine-man's imprecations were relied upon to save the day. Events, too, played into their hands. The Leopard-Chesapeake affair,* in 1807, roused strong feeling in the West and prompted the Governor-General of Canada to begin intrigues looking to an alliance with the redskins in the event of war. And when, late in the same year, Governor Hull of Michigan Territory indiscreetly negotiated a new land cession at Detroit, the northern tribes at once joined Tecumseh's league, muttering threats to slay the chiefs by whom the cession had been sanctioned.

* See "Jefferson and his Colleagues," by Allen Johnson (in "The Chronicles of America").

In the spring of 1808 Tecumseh and his brother carried their plans forward another step by taking up their residence at a point in central Indiana where Tippecanoe Creek flows into the Wabash River. The place - which soon got the name of the Prophet's Town - was almost equidistant from Vincennes, Fort Wayne, and Fort Dearborn; from it the warriors could paddle their canoes to any part of the Ohio or the Mississippi, and with only a short portage, to the waters of the Maumee and the Great Lakes. The situation was, therefore, strategic. A village was laid out, and the population was soon numbered by the hundred. Livestock was acquired, agriculture was begun, the use of whiskey was prohibited, and every indication was afforded of peaceful intent.

Seasoned frontiersmen, however, were suspicious. Reports came in that the Tippecanoe villagers engaged daily in warlike exercises; rumor had it that emissaries of the Prophet were busily stirring the tribes, far and near, to rebellion. Governor Harrison was not a man to be easily frightened, but he became apprehensive, and proposed to satisfy himself by calling Tecumseh into conference.

The interview took place at Vincennes, and was extended over a period of two weeks. There was a show of firmness, yet of good will, on both sides. The Governor counseled peace, orderliness, and industry; the warrior guest professed a desire to be a friend to the United States, but said frankly that if the country continued to deal with the tribes singly in the purchase of land he would be obliged to ally himself with Great Britain. To Harrison's admonition that the redskins should leave off drinking whiskey - "that it was not made for them, but for the white people, who alone knew how to use it" - the visitor replied pointedly by asking that the sale of liquor be stopped.

Notwithstanding the tenseness of the situation, Harrison negotiated the land cessions of 1809, which cost the Indians their last valuable hunting-grounds in Indiana. The powerful Wyandots promptly joined

Tecumseh's league, and war was made inevitable. Delay followed only because the Government at Washington postponed the military occupation of the new purchase, and because the British authorities in Canada, desiring Tecumseh's confederacy to attain its maximum strength before the test came, urged the redskins to wait.

For two more years - while Great Britain and the United States hovered on the brink of war - preparations continued. Tribe after tribe in Indiana and Illinois elected Tecumseh as their chief, alliances reached to regions as remote as Florida. In 1810 another conference took place at Vincennes; and this time, notwithstanding Harrison's request that not more than thirty redskins should attend, four hundred came in Tecumseh's train, fully armed.

"A large portico in front of the Governor's house [says a contemporary account] had been prepared for the purpose with seats, as well for the Indians as for the citizens who were expected to attend. When Tecumseh came from his camp, with about forty of his warriors, he stood off, and on being invited by the Governor, through an interpreter, to take his seat, refused, observing that he wished the council to be held under the shade of some trees in front of the house. When it was objected that it would be troublesome to remove the seats, he replied that 'it would only be necessary to remove those intended for the whites - that the red men were accustomed to sit upon the earth, which was their mother, and that they were always happy to recline upon her bosom.'"*

* James Hall, "Memoir of William Henry Harrison," pp. 113-114.

The chieftain's equivocal conduct aroused fresh suspicion, but he was allowed to proceed with the oration which he had come to deliver. Freely rendered, the speech ran, in part, as follows:

"I have made myself what I am; and I would that I could make the red people as great as the conceptions of my mind, when I think of the Great Spirit that rules over all. I would not then come to Governor Harrison to ask him to tear the treaty [of 1809]; but I would say to him, Brother, you have liberty to return to your own country. Once there was no white man in all this country: then it belonged to red men, children of the same parents, placed on it by the Great Spirit to keep it, to travel over it, to eat its fruits, and fill it with the same race - once a happy race, but now made miserable by the white people, who are never contented, but always encroaching. They have driven us from the great salt water, forced us over the mountains, and would shortly push us into the lakes - but we are determined to go no further. The only way to stop this evil is for all red men to unite in claiming a common and equal right in the land, as it was at first, and should be now - for it never was divided, but belongs to all....Any sale not made by all is not good."

In his reply Harrison declared that the Indians were not one nation, since the Great Spirit had "put six different tongues in their heads," and argued that the Indiana lands had been in all respects properly bought from their rightful owners. Tecumseh's blood boiled under this denial of his main contention, and with the cry, "It is false," he gave a signal to his warriors, who sprang to their feet and seized their war-clubs. For a moment an armed clash was imminent. But Harrison's cool manner enabled him to remain master of the situation, and a well-directed rebuke sent the chieftain and his followers to their quarters.

On the following morning Tecumseh apologized for his impetuosity and asked that the conference be renewed. The request was granted, and again the forest leader pressed for an abandonment of the policy of purchasing land from the separate tribes. Harrison told him that the question was for the President, rather than for, him, to decide. "As the great chief is to determine the matter," responded the visitor grimly, "I hope the Great Spirit will put sense enough into his head to induce him to direct you to give up this land. It is true he is so far off he will not be injured by the war. He may sit still in his town, and drink his wine, while you and I will have to fight it out."

Still the clash was averted. Once more, in the summer of 1811, Tecumseh appeared at Vincennes, and again the deep issue between the two peoples was threshed out as fruitlessly as before. Announcing his purpose to visit the southern tribes to unite them with those of the North in a peaceful confederacy, the chieftain asked that during his absence all matters be left as they were, and promised that upon his return he would go to see President Madison and "settle everything with him."

Naturally, no pledge of the kind was given, and no sooner had Tecumseh and twenty of his warriors started southward on their mission to the Creeks than Harrison began preparations to end the menace that had been so long hanging over the western country. Troops were sent to Harrison; and volunteers were called for. As fast as volunteers came in they were sent up to the Wabash to take possession of the new purchase. Reinforcements arrived from Pittsburgh and from Kentucky, and in a short while the Governor was able to bring together at Fort Harrison, near the site of the present city of Terre Haute, twenty-four companies of regulars, militia, and Indians, aggregating about nine hundred well-armed men.

Late in October this army, commanded by Harrison in person, set forth for the destruction of the Tippecanoe rendezvous. On the way stray redskins were encountered, but the advance was not resisted, and to his surprise Harrison was enabled to lead his forces unmolested to within a few hundred yards of the Prophet's headquarters. Emissaries now came saying that the invasion was wholly unexpected, professing peaceful intentions, and asking for a parley. Harrison had no idea that anything could be settled by negotiation, but he preferred to wait until the next day to make an attack; accordingly he agreed to a council, and the army went into camp for the night on an oak-covered knoll about a mile northwest of the village. No entrenchments were thrown up, but the troops were arranged in a triangle to conform to the contour of the hill, and a hundred sentinels under experienced officers were stationed around the camp-fires. The night was cold, and rain fell at intervals, although at times the moon shone brightly through the flying clouds.

The Governor was well aware of the proneness of the Indians to early morning attacks, so that about four o'clock on the 7th of November he rose to call the men to parade. He had barely pulled on his boots when the forest stillness was broken by the crack of a rifle at the farthest angle of the camp, and instantly the Indian yell, followed by a fusillade, told that a general attack had begun. Before the militiamen could emerge in force from their tents, the sentinel line was broken and the red warriors were pouring into the enclosure. Desperate fighting ensued, and when time for reloading failed, it was rifle butt and bayonet against tomahawk and scalping knife in hand-to-hand combat. For two hours the battle raged in the darkness, and only when daylight came were the troops able to charge the redskins, dislodge them from behind the trees, and drive them to a safe distance in the neighboring swamp. Sixty-one of Harrison's officers and men were killed or mortally wounded; one hundred and twenty-seven others suffered serious injury. The Governor himself probably owed his life to the circumstance that in the confusion he mounted a bay horse instead of his own white stallion, whose rider was shot early in the contest.

The Indian losses were small, and for twenty-four hours Harrison's forces kept their places, hourly expecting another assault. "Night," wrote one of the men subsequently, "found every man mounting guard, without food, fire, or light and in a drizzling rain. The Indian dogs, during the dark hours, produced frequent alarms by prowling in search of carrion about the sentinels." There being no further sign of hostilities, early on the 8th of November a body of mounted riflemen set out for the Prophet's village, which they found deserted. The place had evidently been abandoned in haste, for nothing - not even a fresh stock of English guns and powder - had been destroyed or carried off. After confiscating much-needed provisions and other valuables, Harrison ordered the village to be burned. Then, abandoning camp furniture and private baggage to make room in the wagons for the wounded, he set out on the return trip to Vincennes. A company was left at Fort Harrison, and the main force reached the capital on the 18th of November.

Throughout the western country the news of the battle was received with delight, and it was fondly believed that the backbone of Tecumseh's conspiracy was broken. It was even supposed that the indomitable chieftain and his brother would be forthwith surrendered by the Indians to the authorities of the United States. Harrison was acclaimed as a deliverer. The legislatures of Kentucky, Indiana, and Illinois formally thanked him for his services; and if, as his Federalist enemies charged, he had planned the whole undertaking with a view to promoting his personal fortunes, he ought to have been satisfied with the result. It was the glamour of Tippecanoe that three decades afterwards carried him into the President's chair.

In precipitating a clash while Tecumseh, the mastermind of the fast-growing confederacy, was absent, the Prophet committed a capital blunder. When reproached by his warriors, he declared that all would have gone well but for the fact that on the night before the battle his squaw had profanely touched the pot in which his magic charms were brewed, so that the spell had been broken! The explanation was not very convincing, and ominous murmurings were heard. Before the end of the year, however, word came to Vincennes that the crafty magician was back at Tippecanoe, that the village had been rebuilt, and that the lives of the white settlers who were pouring into the new purchase were again endangered.

Still more alarming was the news of Tecumseh's return in January, 1812, from a very successful visit to the Creeks, Choctaws, and Cherokees. He began by asking leave to make his long-projected visit to Washington to obtain peace from the President, and he professed deep regret for "the unfortunate transaction that took place between the white people and a few of our young men at our village." To the British agent at Amherstburg he declared that had he been on the spot there would have been no fighting at Tippecanoe. It is reasonable to suppose that in this case there would have been, at all events, no Indian attack; for Tecumseh was thoroughly in sympathy with the British plan, which was to unite and arm the natives, but to prevent a premature outbreak. The chieftain's presence, however, would hardly have deterred Harrison from carrying out his decision to break up the Tippecanoe stronghold.

The spring of 1812 brought an ominous renewal of depredations. Two settlers were murdered within three miles of Fort Dearborn; an entire family was massacred but five miles from Vincennes; from all directions came reports of other bloody deeds. The frontier was thrown into panic. A general uprising was felt to be impending; even Vincennes was thought to be in danger. "Most of the citizens of this country," reported Harrison, on the 6th of May, "have abandoned their farms, and taken refuge in such temporary forts as they have been able to construct. Scores fled to Kentucky and to even more distant regions.

Tecumseh continued to assert his friendship for his "white brothers" and to treat the battle at Tippecanoe as a matter of no moment. The murders on the frontier he declared to be the work of the Potawatomi, who were not under his control, and for whose conduct he had no excuse. But it was noted that he made no move to follow up his professed purpose to visit Washington in quest of peace, and that he put forth no effort to restrain his over-zealous allies. It was plain enough that he was simply awaiting a signal from Canada, and that, as the commandant at Fort Wayne tersely reported, if the country should have a war with Great Britain, it must be prepared for an Indian war as well.

Chapter IX.

The War Of 1812 And The New West

The spring of 1812 thus found the back country in a turmoil, and it was with a real sense of relief that the settlers became aware of the American declaration of war against Great Britain on the 18th of June. More than once Governor Harrison had asked for authority to raise an army with which to "scour" the Wabash territory. In the fear that such a step would drive the redskins into the arms of the British, the War Department had withheld its consent. Now that the ban was lifted, the people could expect the necessary measures to be taken for their defense. In no part of the country was the war more popular; nowhere did the mass of the able-bodied population show greater eagerness to take the field.

According to official returns, the Westerners were totally unprepared for the contest. There were but five garrisoned posts between the Ohio and the Canadian frontier. Fort Harrison had fifty men, Fort Wayne eighty-five, Fort Dearborn fifty-three, Fort Mackinac eighty-eight, and Detroit one hundred and twenty - a total force of fewer than four hundred. The entire standing army of the United States numbered but sixty-seven hundred men, and it was obvious that the trans-Alleghany population would be obliged to carry almost alone the burden of their own defense. The task would not be easy; for General Brock, commanding in upper Canada, had at least two thousand regulars and, as soon as hostilities began, was joined by Tecumseh and many hundred redskins.

While the question of the war was still under debate in Congress, President Madison made a requisition on Ohio for twelve hundred militia, and in early summer the Governors of Indiana and Illinois called hundreds of volunteers into service. Leaving their families as far as possible under the protection of stockades or of the towns, the patriots flocked to the mustering-grounds; many, like Cincinnatus of old, deserted the plough in midfield. Guns and ammunition in sufficient quantity were lacking; even tents and blankets were often wanting. But enthusiasm ran high, and only capable leadership was needed to make of these frontier forces, once they were properly equipped, a formidable foe.

The story of the leaders and battles of the war in the West has been told in an earlier volume of this series.* It will be necessary here merely to call to mind the stages through which this contest passed, as a preliminary to a glimpse of the conditions under which Westerners fought and of the new position into which their section of the country was brought when peace was restored. So far as the regions north of the Ohio were concerned, the war developed two phases. The first began with General William Hull's expedition from Ohio against Fort Malden for the relief of Detroit, and it ended with the humiliating surrender of that important post, together with the forced abandonment of Forts Dearborn and Mackinac, so that the Wabash and Maumee became, for all practical purposes, the country's northern boundary. This was a story of complete and bitter defeat. The second phase began likewise with a disaster - the needless loss of a thousand men on the Raisin River, near Detroit. Yet it succeeded in bringing William Henry Harrison into chief command, and it ended in Commodore Perry's signal victory on Lake Erie and Harrison's equally important defeat of the disheartened British land forces on the banks of the Thames River, north of the Lake. At this Battle of the Thames perished Tecumseh, who in point of fact was the real force behind the British campaigns in the West. Tradition describes him on the eve of the battle telling his comrades that his last day had come, solemnly stripping off his British uniform before going into battle, and arraying himself in the fighting costume of his own people.

* See "The Fight for a Free Sea," by Ralph D. Paine (in "The Chronicles of America").

For two-thirds of the time, the war went badly for the Westerners, and only at the end did it turn out to be a brilliant success. The reasons for the dreary succession of disasters are not difficult to discover. Foremost among them is the character of the troops and officers. The material from which the regiments were recruited was intrinsically good, but utterly raw and untrained. The men could shoot well; they had great powers of endurance; and they were brave. But there the list of their military virtues ends.

The scheme of military organization relied upon throughout the West was that of the volunteer militia. In periods of ordinary Indian warfare the system served its purpose fairly well. Under stern necessity, the self-willed, independence-loving backwoodsmen could be brought to act together for a few weeks or months; but they had little systematic training, and their impatience of restraint prevented the building up of any real discipline. There were periodic musters for company or regimental drill. But, as a rule, drill duty was not taken seriously. Numbers of men failed to report; and those who came were likely to give most of their time to horse-races, wrestling-matches, shooting contests - not to mention drinking and brawling – which turned the occasion into mere merrymaking or disorder. The men brought few guns, and when drills were actually held these soldiers in the making contented themselves with parading with cornstalks over their shoulders. "Cornstalk drill" thus became a frontier epithet of derision. It goes without saying that these troops were poorly officered. The captains and colonels were chosen by the men, frequently with more regard for their political affiliations or their general standing in the community than for their capacity as military commanders; nor were the higher officers, appointed by the chief executive of territory, state, or nation, more likely to be chosen with a view to their military fitness.

So it came about, as Roosevelt has said, that the frontier people of the second generation "had no military training whatever, and though they possessed a skeleton militia organization, they derived no benefit from it, because their officers were worthless, and the men had no idea of practising self-restraint or obeying orders longer than they saw fit."* When the War of 1812 began, these backwoods troops were pitted against British regulars who were powerfully supported by Indian allies. The officers of these untrained American troops were, like Hull, pompous, broken-down, political incapables; while to the men themselves may fairly be applied Amos Kendall's disgusted characterization of a Kentucky muster: "The soldiers are under no more restraint than a herd of swine. Reasoning, remonstrating, threatening, and ridiculing their officers, they show their sense of equality and their total want of subordination." Not until the very last of the war, when under Harrison's direction capable and experienced officers drilled them into real soldiers, did these backwoods stalwarts become an effective fighting force.

* "Winning of the West," vol. IV, p. 246.

There were also shortcomings of another sort. None was more exasperating or costly than the lack of means of transportation. Even in Ohio, the oldest and most settled portion of the Northwest, roads were few and poor; elsewhere there were practically none of any kind. But the regions in which the war was carried on were far too sparsely populated to be able to furnish the supplies, even the foodstuffs, needed by the troops; and materials of every sort had to be transported from the East, by river, lake, and wilderness trail. Up and down the great unbroken stretches between the Ohio and the Lakes moved the floundering supply trains in the vain effort to keep up with the armies, or to reach camps or forts in time to avert starvation or disaster. Pack-horses waded knee-deep in mud; wagons were dragged through mire up to their hubs; even empty vehicles sometimes became so embedded that they had to be abandoned, the drivers being glad to get off with their horses alive. Many times a quartermaster, taking advantage of a frost, would send off a convoy of provisions, only to hear of its being swamped by a thaw before reaching its destination. One of the tragedies of the war was the suffering of the troops while waiting for supplies of clothing, tents, medicines, and food which were stuck in swamps or frozen up in rivers or lakes.

Beset with pleurisy, pneumonia, and rheumatism in winter, with fevers in summer, and subject to attack by the Indians at all times, these frontier soldiers led an existence of exceptional hardship. Only the knowledge that they were fighting for their freedom and their homes held them to their task. An interesting sidelight on the conditions under which their work was done is contained in the following extract from a letter written by a volunteer in 1814:

"On the second day of our march a courier arrived from General Harrison, ordering the artillery to advance with all possible speed. This was rendered totally impossible by the snow which took place, it being a complete swamp nearly all day. On the evening of the same day news arrived that General Harrison had retreated to Portage River, eighteen miles in the rear of the encampment at the rapids. As many men as could be spared determined to proceed immediately to re-enforce him.... At two o'clock the next morning our tents were struck, and in half an hour we were on the road. I will candidly confess that on that day I regretted being a soldier. On that day we marched thirty miles under an incessant rain; and I am afraid you will doubt my veracity when I tell you that in eight miles of the best of the road, it took us over the knees, and often to the middle. The Black Swamp would have been considered impassable by all but men determined to surmount every difficulty to accomplish the object of their march. In this swamp you lose sight of terra firma altogether - the water was about six inches deep on the ice, which was very rotten, often breaking through to the depth of four or five feet. The same night we encamped on very wet ground, but the driest that could be found, the rain still continuing. It was with difficulty we could raise fires; we had no tents; our clothes were wet, no axes, nothing to cook with, and very little to eat. A brigade of pack-horses being near us, we procured from them some flour, killed a hog (there were plenty of THEM along the road); our bread was baked in the ashes, and our pork we broiled on the coals - a sweeter meal I never partook of. When we went to sleep it was on two logs laid close to each other, to keep our bodies from the damp ground. Good God! What a pliant being is man in adversity.*

* Dawson. "William H. Harrison," p. 369.

The principal theater of war was the Great Lakes and the lands adjacent to them. Prior to the campaign which culminated in Jackson's victory at New Orleans after peace had been signed, the Mississippi Valley had been untrodden by British soldiery. The contest, none the less, came close home to the backwoods populations. Scores of able-bodied men from every important community saw months or years of toilsome service; many failed to return to their homes, or else returned crippled, weakened, or stricken with fatal diseases; crops were neglected, or had only such care as could be given them by old men and boys; trade languished; Indian depredations wrought further ruin to life and property and kept the people continually in alarm. Until 1814, reports of successive defeats, in both the East and West, had a depressing influence and led to solemn speculation as to whether the back country stood in danger of falling again under British dominion.

It was, therefore, with a very great sense of relief that the West heard in 1815 that peace had been concluded. At a stroke both the British menace and the danger from the Indians were removed; for although the redskins were still numerous and discontented, their spirit of resistance was broken. Never again was there a general uprising against the whites; never again did the Northwest witness even a local Indian war of any degree of seriousness save Black Hawk's Rebellion in 1832. Tecumseh manifestly realized before he made his last stand at the Thames that the cause of his people was forever lost.

For several years the unsettled conditions on the frontiers had restrained any general migration thither from the seaboard States. But within a few months after the proclamation of peace the tide again set westward, and with an unprecedented force. Men who had suffered in their property or other interests from the war turned to Indiana and Illinois as a promising field in which to rebuild their fortunes. The rapid extinction of Indian titles opened up vast tracts of desirable land, and the conditions of purchase were made so easy that any man of ordinary industry and integrity could meet them. Speculators and promoters industriously advertised the advantages of localities in which they were interested, boomed new towns, and even loaned money to ambitious emigrants.

The upshot was that the population of Indiana grew from twenty-five thousand in 1810 to seventy thousand in 1816, when the State was admitted to the Union. Illinois filled with equal rapidity, and attained statehood only two years later. Then the tide swept irresistibly westward across the Mississippi into the great regions which had been acquired from France in

1803. As late as 1819, the Territory of Missouri, comprising all of the Louisiana Purchase north of the present State of Louisiana, had a population of only twenty-two thousand, including many French and Spanish settlers and traders. But in 1818 it had a population of more than sixty thousand, and was asking Congress for legislation under which the most densely inhabited portion should be set off as the State of Missouri. Thus the Old Northwest was not merely losing its frontier character and taking its place in the nation on a footing with the seaboard sections; it was also serving as the open gateway to a newer, vaster, and in some respects richer American back country.

In the main, southern Indiana and Illinois - as well as the trans-Mississippi territory - drew from Kentucky, Tennessee, Virginia, and the remoter South. North of the latitude of Indianapolis and St. Louis the lines of migration led chiefly from New England, New York, and Pennsylvania. But many of the settlers came, immediately or after only a brief interval, from Europe. The decade following the close of the war was a time of unprecedented emigration from England, Scotland, Ireland, and Germany to the United States; and while many of the newcomers found homes in the eastern States, where they in a measure offset the depopulation caused by the westward exodus, a very large proportion pressed on across the mountains in quest of the cheap lands in the undeveloped interior. During these years the western country was repeatedly visited by European travelers with a view to ascertaining its resources, markets, and other attractions for settlers; and emigration thither was powerfully stimulated by the writings of these observers, as well as by the activities of sundry founders of agricultural colonies.

"These favorable accounts," wrote Adlard Welby, an Englishman who made a tour of inspection through the West in 1819, "aided by a period of real privation and discontent in Europe, caused emigration to increase tenfold; and though various reports of unfavorable nature soon circulated, and many who had emigrated actually returned to their native land in disgust, yet still the trading vessels were filled with passengers of all ages and descriptions, full of hope, looking forward to the West as to a land of liberty and delight - a land flowing with milk and honey - a second land of Canaan.*

* Thwaites, "Early Western Travels," vol. XII, p. 148.

After the dangers from the Indians were overcome, the main obstacle to western development was the lack of means of easy and cheap transportation. The settler found it difficult to reach the Legion which he had selected for his home. Eastern supplies of salt, iron, hardware, and fabrics and foodstuffs could be obtained only at great expense. The fast-increasing products of the western farms - maize, wheat, meats, livestock - could be marketed only at a cost which left a slender margin of profit. The experiences of the late war had already proved the need of highways as auxiliaries of national defense. It required a month to carry goods from Baltimore to central Ohio. None the less, even before the War of 1812, hundreds of transportation companies were running four-horse freight wagons between the eastern and western States; and in 1820 more than three thousand wagons - practically all carrying western products - passed back and forth between Philadelphia and Pittsburgh, transporting merchandise valued at eighteen million dollars.

Small wonder that western producer and eastern dealer alike became interested in internal improvements; or that under the double stimulus of private and public enterprise Indian trails fast gave way to rough pioneer roadways, and they to carefully planned and durable turnpikes. Long before the War of 1812, Jefferson, Gallatin, Clay, and other statesmen had conceived of a great highway, or series of highways, connecting the seaboard with the interior as the surest and best means of promoting national unity and strength; and, in the act of Congress of 1802 admitting the State of Ohio, a promising beginning had been made by setting aside five per cent of the money received from the sale of public lands in the State for the building of roads extending eastward to the navigable waters of Atlantic streams. In 1808 Secretary Gallatin had presented to Congress a report calling for an outlay on internal improvements of two million dollars of federal money a year for ten years; and in 1811 the Government had entered upon the greatest undertaking of its kind in the history of the country.

This enterprise was the building of the magnificent highway known to the law as the Cumberland Road, but familiar to uncounted emigrants, travelers, and traders - and deeply embedded in the traditions of the Middle States and the West - as the National Road. Starting at Cumberland, Maryland, this great artery of commerce and travel was pushed slowly through the Alleghanies, even in the dark days of the war, and by 1818 it was open for traffic as far west as Wheeling. The method of construction was that which had lately been devised by John McAdam in England, and involved spreading crushed limestone over a carefully prepared road-bed in three layers, traffic being permitted for a time over each layer in succession. This "macadamized" surface was curved to permit drainage, and extra precautions were taken in localities where spring freshets were likely to cause damage.

Controversy raged over proposals to extend the road to the farthest West, to provide its upkeep by a system of tolls, and to build similar highways farther north and south. But for a time constitutional and legal difficulties were swept aside and construction continued. Columbus was reached in 1833, Indianapolis about 1840; and the roadway was graded to Vandalia, then the capital of Illinois, and marked out to Jefferson City, Missouri, although it was never completed to the last-mentioned point by federal authority. When one reads that the original cost of construction mounted to $10,000 a mile in central Pennsylvania, and even $13,000 a mile in the neighborhood of Wheeling, one's suspicion is aroused that public contracts were not less dubious a hundred years ago than they have been known to be in our own time.

The National Road has long since lost its importance as the great connecting link of East and West. But in its day, especially before 1860, it was a teeming thoroughfare. Its course was lined with hospitable farmhouses and was dotted with fast-growing villages and towns. Some of the latter which once were nationally famed were left high and dry by later shifts of the lines of traffic, and have quite disappeared from the map. Throughout the spring and summer months there was a steady westward stream of emigrants; hardly a day failed to bring before the observer's eye the creaking canvas-covered wagon of the homeseeker. Singly and in companies they went, ever toward the promised land. Wagon-trains of merchandise from the eastern markets toiled patiently along the way.

Speculators, peddlers, and sightseers added to the procession, and in hundreds of farmhouses the womenfolk and children gathered in interested groups by the evening fire to hear the chance visitor talk politics or war and retail with equal facility the gossip of the next township and that of Washington or New York. Great stage-coach lines - the National Road Stage Company, the Ohio National Stage Company, and others - advertised the advantages of their services and sought patronage with all the ingenuity of the modern railroad. Taverns and roadhouses of which no trace remains today offered entertainment at any figure, and of almost any character, that the customer desired. Eastward flowed a steady stream of wagon-trains of flour, tobacco, and pork, with great droves of cattle and hogs to be fattened for the Philadelphia or Baltimore markets.

At almost precisely the same time that the first shovelful of earth was turned for the Cumberland Road, people dwelling on the banks of the upper Ohio were startled by the spectacle of a large boat moving majestically down stream entirely devoid of sail, oar, pole, or any other visible means of propulsion or control. This object of wonderment was the New Orleans, the first steamboat to be launched on western waters.

The conquest of the steamboat was speedy and complete. Already in 1819 there were sixty-three such craft on the Ohio, and in 1834 - when the total shipping tonnage, of the Atlantic seaboard was 76,064, and of the British Empire 82,696 - the tonnage afloat on the Ohio and Mississippi was 126,278. Vessels regularly ascended the navigable tributaries of the greater streams in quest of cargoes, and while craft of other sorts did not disappear, the great and growing commerce of the river was revolutionized.

In the upbuilding of steamboat navigation the thriving, bustling, boastful spirit of the West found ample play. Steamboat owners vied with one another in adorning their vessels with bowsprits, figureheads, and all manner of tinseled decorations, and in providing elegant accommodations for passengers; engineers and pilots gloried in speed records and challenged one another to races which ended in some of the most shocking steamboat disasters known to history. The unconscious bombast of an anonymous Cincinnati writer in Timothy Flint's "Western Monthly Review" in 1827 gives us the real flavor of the steamboat business on the threshold of the Jacksonian era:

"An Atlantic cit, who talks of us under the name of backwoodsmen, would not believe, that such fairy structures of oriental gorgeousness and splendor as the Washington, the Florida, the Walk in the Water, The Lady of the Lake, etc., etc., had ever existed in the imaginative brain of a romancer, much less, that they were actually in existence, rushing down the Mississippi, as on the wings of the wind, or plowing up between the forests, and walking against the mighty current 'as things of life,' bearing speculators, merchants, dandies, fine ladies, everything real, and everything affected, in the form of humanity, with pianos, and stocks of novels, and cards, and dice, and flirting, and love-making, and drinking, and champagne, and on the deck, perhaps, three hundred fellows, who have seen alligators, and neither fear whiskey, nor gun-powder. A steamboat, coming from New Orleans, brings to the remotest villages of our streams, and the very doors of the cabins, a little Paris, a section of Broadway, or a slice of Philadelphia, to ferment in the minds of our young people, the innate propensity for fashions and finery....Cincinnati will soon be the centre of the "celestial empire," as the Chinese say; and instead of encountering the storms, the seasickness, and dangers of a passage from the Gulf of Mexico to the Atlantic, whenever the Erie Canal shall be completed, the opulent southern planters will take their families, their dogs and parrots, through a world of forests, from New Orleans to New York, giving us a call by the way. When they are more acquainted with us, their voyage will often terminate here."*

* Vol. I., p. 25 (May, 1827).

The new West was frankly materialistic. Yet its interests were by no means restricted to steamboats, turnpikes, crops, exports, and moneymaking. It concerned itself much with religion. One of the most familiar figures on trail and highway was the circuit-rider, with his Bible and saddlebags; and no community was so remote, or so hardened, as not to be raised occasionally to a frenzy of religious zeal by the crude but terrifying eloquence of the revivalist. For education, likewise, there was a growing regard. Nowhere did the devotion of the Western people to the twin ideas of democracy and enlightenment find nobler expression than in the clause of the Indiana constitution of 1816 making it the duty of the Legislature to provide for "a general system of education, ascending in a regular gradation from township schools to a state university, wherein tuition shall be gratis, and equally open to all." This principle found general application throughout the Northwest. By 1830 common schools existed wherever population was sufficient to warrant the expense; academies and other secondary schools were springing up in Cincinnati, Louisville, St. Louis, and many lesser places; state universities existed in Ohio and Indiana; and Baptists, Methodists, and Presbyterians had begun to dot the country with small colleges. Literature developed slowly. But newspapers appeared almost before there were readers; and that the new society was by no means without cultural, and even aesthetic, aspiration is indicated by the long-continued rivalry of Cincinnati and Lexington, Kentucky, to be known as "the Athens of the West."

Chapter X.

Sectional Cross Currents

The War of 1812 did much in America to stimulate national pride and to foster a sense of unity. None the less, the decade following the Peace of Ghent proved the beginning of a long era in which the point of view in politics, business, and social life was distinctly sectional. New England, the Middle States, the South, the West all were bent upon getting the utmost advantages from their resources; all were viewing public questions in the light of their peculiar interests. In the days of Clay and Calhoun and Jackson the nation's politics were essentially a struggle for power among the sections.

There was a time when the frontier folk of the trans-Alleghany country from Lakes to Gulf were much alike. New Englanders in the Reserve, Pennsylvanians in central Ohio, Virginians and Carolinians in Kentucky and southern Indiana, Georgians in Alabama and Mississippi, Kentuckians and Tennesseeans in Illinois and Missouri - all were pioneer farmers and stock-raiser's, absorbed in the conquest of the wilderness and all thinking, working, and living in much the same way. but by 1820 the situation had altered. The West was still a "section," whose interests and characteristics contrasted sharply with those of

New England or the Middle States. Yet upon occasion it could act with very great effect, as for instance when it rallied to the support of Jackson and bore him triumphantly to the presidential chair. Great divergences, however, had grown up within this western area; differences which had existed from the beginning had been brought into sharp relief. Under play of climatic and industrial forces, the West had itself fallen apart into sections.

Foremost was the cleavage between North and South, on a line marked roughly by the Ohio River. Climate, soil, the cotton gin, and slavery combined to make of the southern West a great cotton-raising area, interested in the same things and swayed by the same impulses as the southern seaboard. Similarly, economic conditions combined to make of the northern West a land of small farmers, free labor, town-building, and diversified manufactures and trade. A very large chapter of American history hinges on this wedging apart of Southwest and Northwest. To this day the two great divisions have never wholly come together in their ways of thinking.

But neither of these western segments was itself entirely a unit. The Northwest, in particular, had been settled by people drawn from every older portion of the country, and as the frontier receded and society took on a more matured aspect, differences of habits and ideas were accentuated rather than obscured. Men can get along very well with one another so long as they live apart and do not try to regulate their everyday affairs on common lines.

The great human streams that poured into the Northwest flowed from two main sources - the nearer

South and New England. Ohio, Indiana, and Illinois were first peopled by men and women of Southern stock. Some migrated directly from Virginia, the Carolinas, and even Georgia. But most came from Kentucky and Tennessee and represented the second generation of white people in those States, now impelled to move on to a new frontier by the desire for larger and cheaper farms. Included in this Southern element were many representatives of the well-to-do classes, who were drawn to the new territories by the opportunity for speculation in land and for political preferment, and by the opening which the fast-growing communities afforded for lawyers, doctors, and members of other professions. The number of these would have been larger had there been less rigid restrictions upon slaveholding. It was rather, however, the poorer whites - the more democratic, non-slave-holding Southern element - that formed the bulk of the earlier settlers north of the Ohio.

There was much westward migration from New England before the War of 1812, but only a small share of it reached the Ohio country, and practically none went beyond the Western Reserve. The common goal was western New York. Here again there was some emigration of the well-to-do and influential. But, as in the South, the people who moved were mainly those who were having difficulty in making ends meet and who could see no way of bettering their condition in their old homes. The back country of Maine, New Hampshire, Vermont, and western Massachusetts was filled with people of this sort - poor, discontented, restless, without political influence, and needing only the incentive of cheap lands in the West to sever the slender ties which bound them to the stony hillsides of New England.

After 1815 New England emigration rose to astonishing proportions, and an increasing number of the homeseekers passed - directly or after a sojourn in the Lower Lake country of New York - into the Northwest. The opening of the Erie Canal in 1825 made the westward journey easier and cheaper. The routes of travel led to Lakes Ontario and Erie, thence to the Reserve in northern Ohio, thence by natural stages into other portions of northern Ohio, Indiana, and Illinois, and eventually into southern Michigan and Wisconsin. Not until after 1830 did the stalwart homeseekers penetrate north of Detroit; the great stretches of prairie between Lakes Erie and Michigan, and to the south - left quite untouched by Southern pioneers - satisfied every desire of these restless farmers from New England.

For a long time Southerners determined the course of history in the Old Northwest. They occupied the field first, and they had the great advantage of geographical proximity to their old homes. Furthermore, they lived more compactly; the New Englanders were not only spread over the broader prairie stretches of the north, but scattered to some extent throughout the entire region between the Lakes and the Ohio.* But by the middle of the century not only had the score of northern counties been inundated by the "Yankees" but the waves were pushing far into the interior, where they met and mingled with the counter-current. Both Illinois and Indiana became, in a preeminent degree, melting-pots in which was fused by slow and sometimes painful processes an amalgam which Bryce and other keen observers have pronounced the most American thing in America.

* In 1820 the population of Indiana was confined

almost entirely to the southern third of the State, although the removal of the capital, in 1825, from Corydon to Indianapolis was carried out in the confidence that eventually that point would become the State's populational as it was its geographical center. When, in 1818, Illinois was admitted to the Union its population was computed at 40,000. The figure was probably excessive; at all events, contemporaries testify that so eager were the people for statehood that many were counted twice, and even emigrants were counted as they passed through the Territory. But the census of 1880 showed a population of 55,000, settled almost wholly in the southern third of the State, with narrow tongues of inhabited land stretching up the river valleys toward the north. Two slave States flanked the southern end of the commonwealth; almost half of its area lay south of a westward prolongation of Mason and Dixon's line. Save for a few Pennsylvanians, the people were Southern; the State was for all practical purposes a Southern State. As late as 1883 the Legislature numbered fifty-eight members from the South, nineteen from the Middle States, and only four from New England.

Of the great national issues in the quarter-century following the War of 1812 there were some upon which people of the Northwest, in spite of their differing points of view, could very well agree. Internal improvement was one of these. Roads and canals were necessary outlets to southern and eastern markets, and any reasonable proposal on this subject could be assured of the Northwest's solid support. The thirty-four successive appropriations to 1844 for the Cumberland Road, Calhoun's "Bonus Bill" of 1816, the bill of 1822 authorizing a continuous national jurisdiction over the Cumberland Road, the comprehensive

"Survey Bill" of 1824, the Maysville Road Bill of 1830 - all were backed by the united strength of the Northwestern senators and representatives.

So with the tariff. The cry of the East for protection to infant industries was echoed by the struggling manufacturers of Cincinnati, Louisville, and other towns; while a protective tariff as a means of building up the home market for foodstuffs and raw materials seemed to the Westerner an altogether reasonable and necessary expedient. Ohio alone in the Northwest had an opportunity to vote on the protective bill of 1816, and gave its enthusiastic support. Ohio, Indiana, and Illinois voted unitedly for the bills of 1820, 1824, 1828, and 1832. The principal western champion of the protective policy was Henry Clay, a Kentuckian; but the Northwest supported the policy more consistently than did Clay's own State and section.

On the National Bank the position of the Northwest was no less emphatic. The people were little troubled by the question of constitutionality; but believing that the bank was an engine of tyranny in the hands of an eastern aristocracy, they were fully prepared to support Jackson in his determination to extinguish that "un-American monopoly."

There were other subjects upon which agreement was reached either with difficulty or not at all. One of these was the form of local government which should be adopted. Southerners and New Englanders brought to their new homes widely differing political usages. The former were accustomed to the county as the principal local unit of administration. It was a relatively large division, whose affairs were managed by elective officers, mainly a board of commissioners. The New

Englanders, on the other hand, had grown up under the town-meeting system and clung to the notion that an indispensable feature of democratic local government is the periodic assembling of the citizens of a community for legislative, fiscal, and electoral purposes. The Illinois constitution of 1818 was made by Southerners, and naturally it provided for the county system. But protest from the "Yankee" elements became so strong that in the new constitution of 1848 provision was made for township organization wherever the people of a county wanted it; and this form of government, at first prevalent only in the northern counties, is now found in most of the central and southern counties as well.

The most deeply and continuously dividing issue in the Northwest, as in the nation, at large, was negro slavery. Although written by Southern men, the Ordinance of 1787 stipulated that there should be "neither slavery nor involuntary servitude in the said territory, otherwise than in the punishment of crimes whereof the party shall have been duly convicted." If the government of the Northwest had been one of laws, and not of men, this specific provision would have made the territory free soil and would have relieved the inhabitants from all interest in the "peculiar institution." But the laws never execute themselves - least of all in frontier communities. In point of fact, considerable numbers of slaves were held in the territory until the nineteenth century was far advanced. As late as 1830 thirty-two negroes were held in servitude in the single town of Vincennes. Slavery could and did prevail to a limited extent because existing property rights were guaranteed in the Ordinance itself, in the deed of cession by Virginia, in the Jay Treaty of 1794, and in other fundamental acts.

The courts of the Northwest held that slave-owners whose property could be brought under any of these guarantees might retain that property; and although no court countenanced further importation, itinerant Southerners - rich planters traveling in their family carriages, with servants, packs of hunting-dogs, and trains of slaves, their nightly camp-fires lighting up the wilderness where so recently the Indian hunter had held possession" - occasionally settled in southern Indiana or Illinois and with the connivance of the authorities kept some of their dependents in slavery, or quasi-slavery, for decades.

Of actual slaveholders there were not enough to influence public sentiment greatly. But the people of Southern extraction, although neither slave holders nor desiring to become such, had no strong moral convictions on the subject. Indeed, they were likely to feel that the anti-slavery restriction imposed an unfortunate impediment in the way of immigration from the South. Hence the persistent demand of citizens of Indiana and Illinois for a relaxation of the drastic prohibition of slavery in the Ordinance of 1787. In 1796 Congress was petitioned from Kaskaskia to extend relief; in 1799 the territorial Legislature was urged to bring about a repeal; in 1802 an Indiana territorial convention at Vincennes memorialized Congress in behalf of a suspension of the proviso for a period of ten years. Not only were violations of the law winked at, but both Indiana and Illinois deliberately built up a system of indenture which partook strongly of the characteristics of slavery. After much controversy, Indiana, in 1816, framed a state constitution which reiterated the language of the Northwest Ordinance, but without invalidating titles to existing slave property; while Illinois was admitted to the

Union in 1818 with seven or eight hundred slaves upon her soil, and with a constitution which continued the old system of indenture with slight modification.

In a heated contest in Illinois in 1824 over the question of calling a state convention to draft a constitution legalizing slavery the people of Northern antecedents made their votes tell and defeated the project. But, like other parts of the Northwest, this State never became a unit on the slavery issue. Certainly it never became abolitionist. By an almost unanimous vote the Legislature, in 1837, adopted joint resolutions which condemned abolitionism as "more productive of evil than of moral and political good"; and in Congress in the preceding year the delegation of the State had given solid support to the "gag resolutions," which were intended to deny a hearing to all petitions on the slavery question.

Throughout the great era of slavery controversy the Northwest was prolific of schemes of compromise, for the constant clash of Northern and Southern elements developed an aptitude for settlement by agreement on moderate lines. The people of the section as a whole long clung to popular, or "squatter," sovereignty as the supremely desirable solution of the slavery question - a device formulated and defended by two of the Northwest's own statesmen, Cass and Douglas, and relinquished only slowly and reluctantly under the leadership, not of a New England abolitionist, but of a statesman of Southern birth who had come to the conclusion that the nation could not permanently exist half slave and half free.

Cass, Douglas, Lincoln - all were adopted sons of the Northwest, and the career of every one illustrates not only the prodigality with which the back country showered its opportunities upon men of industry and talent, but the play and interplay of sectional and social forces in the building of the newer nation. Cass and Douglas were New Englanders. One was born at Exeter, New Hampshire, in 1782; the other at Brandon, Vermont, in 1813. Lincoln sprang from Virginian and Kentuckian stocks. His father's family moved from Virginia to Kentucky at the close of the Revolution; in 1784 his grandfather was killed by lurking Indians, and his father, then a boy of six, was saved from captivity only by a lucky shot of an older brother. Lincoln himself was born in 1809. Curiously enough, Cass and Douglas, the New Englanders, played their roles on the national stage as Jackson Democrats, while Lincoln, the Kentuckian of Virginian ancestry, became a Whig and later a Republican.

Cass and Douglas were well-born. Cass's father was a thrifty soldier-farmer who made for his family a comfortable home at Zanesville, Ohio; Douglas's father was a successful physician. Lincoln was born in obscurity and wretchedness. His father, Thomas Lincoln, was a ne'er-do-well Kentucky carpenter, grossly illiterate, unable or unwilling to rise above the lowest level of existence in the pioneer settlements. His mother, Nancy Hanks, whatever her antecedents may have been, was a woman of character, and apparently of some education. But she died when her son was only nine years of age.

Cass and Douglas had educational opportunities which in their day were exceptional. Both attended famous academies and received instruction in the classics, mathematics, and philosophy. Both grew up in an environment of enlightenment and integrity. Lincoln, on the other hand, got a few weeks of instruction under two amateur teachers in Kentucky and a few months more in Indiana - in all, hardly as much as one year; and as a boy he knew only rough, coarse surroundings. When, in 1816, the restless head of the family moved from Kentucky to southern Indiana, his worldly belongings consisted of a parcel of carpenters' tools and cooking utensils, a little bedding, and about four hundred gallons of whiskey. No one who has not seen the sordidness, misery, and apparent hopelessness of the life of the "poor whites" even today, in the Kentucky and southern Indiana hills, can fully comprehend the chasm which separated the boy Lincoln from every sort of progress and distinction.

All three men prepared for public life by embracing the profession that has always, in this country, proved the surest avenue to preferment - the law. But, whereas Cass arrived at maturity just in time to have an active part in the War of 1812, and in this way to make himself the most logical selection for the governorship of the newly organized Michigan Territory, Douglas saw no military service, and Lincoln only a few weeks of service during the Black Hawk War, and both were obliged to seek fame and fortune along the thorny road of politics. Following admission to the bar at Jacksonville, Illinois, in 1834, Douglas was elected public prosecutor of the first judicial circuit in 1835; elected to the state Legislature in 1836; appointed by President Van Buren registrar of the land office at Springfield in 1837; made a judge of the supreme court of the State in 1841; and elected to the national House of Representatives in 1843. Resourceful, skilled in debate, intensely patriotic, and favored with many winning personal qualities, he drew to himself men of both Northern and Southern proclivities and became an influential exponent of broad and enduring nationalism.

Meanwhile, after a first defeat, Lincoln was elected to the Illinois Legislature in 1834, and again in 1836. When he gathered all of his worldly belongings in a pair of saddlebags and fared forth to the new capital, Springfield, to settle himself to the practice of law, he had more than a local reputation for oratorical power; and events were to prove that he had not only facility in debate and familiarity with public questions, but incomparable devotion to lofty principles. In the subsequent unfolding of the careers of Lincoln and Douglas - especially in the turn of events that brought to each a nomination for the presidency by a great party in 1860 - there was no small amount of good luck and sheer accident. But it is equally true that by prodigious effort Kentuckian and Vermonter alike hewed out their own ways to greatness.

It was the glory of the Northwest to offer a competence to the needy, the baffled, the discouraged, the tormented of the eastern States and of Europe. The bulk of its fast-growing population consisted, it is true, of ordinary folk who could have lived on in fair comfort in the older sections, yet who were ambitious to own more land, to make more money, and to secure larger advantages for their children. But nowhere else was the road for talent so wide open, entirely irrespective of inheritance, possessions, education, environment. Nowhere outside of the trans-Alleghany country would the rise of a Lincoln have been possible.

Chapter XI.

The Upper Mississippi Valley

While the Ohio country - the lower half of the States of Ohio, Indiana, and Illinois - was throwing off its frontier character, the remoter Northwest was still a wilderness frequented only by fur-traders and daring explorers. And that far Northwest by the sources of the Mississippi had been penetrated by few white men since the seventeenth century. The earliest white visitors to the upper Mississippi are not clearly known. They may have been Pierre Radisson and his brother-in-law, Menard des Grosseilliers, who are alleged to have covered the long portage from Lake Superior to the Mississippi in or about 1665; but the matter rests entirely on how one interprets Radisson's vague account of their western perambulations. At all events, in 1680 - seven years after the descent of the river from the Wisconsin to the Arkansas by Marquette and Joliet - Louis Hennepin, under instructions from La Salle, explored the stream from the mouth of the Illinois to the Falls of St. Anthony, where the city of Minneapolis now stands, five hundred miles from the true source.

There the matter of exploration rested until the days of Thomas Jefferson, when the purchase of Louisiana lent fresh interest to northwestern geography. In 1805 General James Wilkinson, in military command in the

West, dispatched Lieutenant Zebulon M. Pike with a party of twenty men from St. Louis to explore the headwaters of the great river, make peace with the Indians, and select sites for fortified posts. From his winter quarters near the Falls, Pike pushed northward over the snow and ice until, early in 1806, he reached Leech Lake, in Cass County, Minnesota, which he wrongly took to be the source of the Father of Waters. It is little wonder that, at a time when the river and lake surfaces were frozen over and the whole country heavily blanketed with snow, he should have found it difficult to disentangle the maze of streams and lakes which fill the low-lying region around the headwaters of the Mississippi, the Red River, and the Lake of the Woods. In 1820 General Cass, Governor of Michigan, which then had the Mississippi for its western boundary, led an expedition into the same region as far as Cass Lake, where the Indians told him that the true source lay some fifty miles to the northwest. It remained for the traveler and ethnologist Henry Schoolcraft, twelve years later, to discover Lake Itasca, in modern Clearwater County, which occupies a depression near the center of the rock-rimmed basin in which the river takes its rise.

It was not these infrequent explorers, however, who opened paths for pioneers into the remote Northwest, but traders in. search of furs and pelts - those commercial pathfinders of western civilization. There is scarcely a town or city in the State of Wisconsin that does not owe its origin, directly or indirectly, to these men. Cheap and tawdry enough were the commodities bartered for these wonderful beaver and otter pelts - ribbons and gewgaws, looking-glasses and combs, blankets and shawls of gaudy color. But scissors and knives, gunpowder and shot, tobacco and whiskey, went also in the traders' packs, though traffic in firewater was forbidden. These goods, upon arrival at Mackinac, were sent out by canoes and bateaux to the different posts, where they were dealt out to the savages directly or were dispatched to the winter camps along the far-reaching waterways." Returning home in the spring, the bucks would set their squaws and children at making maple sugar or planting corn, watermelons, potatoes, and squash, while they themselves either dawdled their time away or hunted for summer furs. In the autumn, the wild rice was garnered along the sloughs and the river mouths, and the straggling field crops were gathered in - some of the product being hidden in skillfully covered pits, as a reserve, and some dried for transportation in the winter's campaign. The villagers were now ready to depart for their hunting-grounds, often hundreds of miles away. It was then that the trader came and credits were wrangled over and extended, each side endeavoring to get the better of the other."*

* Thwaites, "Story of Wisconsin," p. 156.

This traffic was largely managed by the British in Canada until 1816, when an act of Congress forbade foreign traders to operate on United States soil. But a heavier blow was inflicted in the establishment of John Jacob Astor's American Fur Company, which was given a substantial monopoly of Indian commerce. From its headquarters on Mackinac Island this great corporation rapidly squeezed the clandestine British agents out of the American trade, introduced improved methods, and built up a system which covered the entire fur-bearing Northwest.

Of this remoter Northwest, the region between Lakes

Erie and Michigan was the most accessible from the East; yet it was avoided by the first pioneers, who labored under a strange misapprehension about its climate and resources. In spite of the fact that it abounded in rich bottom-lands and fertile prairies and was destined to become one of the most bountiful orchards of the world, it was reported by early prospectors to be swampy and unfit for cultivation. Though Governor Cass did his best to overcome this prejudice, for years settlers preferred to gather mainly about Detroit, leaving the rich interior to fur-traders. When enlightenment eventually came, population poured in with a rush. Detroit - which was a village in 1820 - became ten years later a thriving city of thirty thousand and the western terminus of a steamboat line from Buffalo, which year after year multiplied its traffic. By the year 1837 the great territory lying east of Lake Michigan was ready for statehood.

Almost simultaneously the region to the west of Lake Michigan began to emerge from the fur-trading stage. The place of the picturesque trader, however, was not taken at once by the prosaic farmer. The next figure in the pageant was the miner. The presence of lead in the stretch of country between the Wisconsin and Illinois rivers was known to the Indians before the coming of the white man, but they began to appreciate its value only after the introduction of firearms by the French. The ore lay at no great depth in the Galena limestone, and the aborigines collected it either by stripping it from the surface or by sinking shallow shafts from which it was hoisted, in deerskin bags. Shortly after the War of 1812 American prospectors pushed into the region, and the Government began granting leases on easy terms to operators. In 1823 one of these men arrived with soldiers, supplies, skilled miners, and one hundred and fifty slaves; and thereafter the "diggings" fast became a mecca for miners, smelters, speculators, merchants, gamblers, and get-rich-quick folk of every sort, who swarmed thither by thousands from every part of the United States, especially the South, and even from Europe. "Mushroom towns sprang up all over the district; deep-worn native paths became ore roads between the burrows and the river-landings; sink-holes abandoned by the Sauk and Foxes, when no longer to be operated with their crude tools, were reopened and found to be exceptionally rich, while new diggings and smelting-furnaces, fitted out with modern appliances, fairly dotted the map of the country."*

* Thwaites, "Story of Wisconsin". p. 163.

Galena was the entrepot of the region. A trail cut thither from Peoria soon became a well-worn coach road; roads were early opened to Chicago and Milwaukee. In 1822 Galena was visited by a Mississippi River steamboat, and a few years later regular steamboat traffic was established. And it was by these roadways and waterways that homeseekers soon began to arrive.

The invasion of the white man, accompanied though it was by treaties, was bitterly resented by the Indian tribes who occupied the Northwest above the Illinois River. These Sioux, Sauk and Foxes, and Winnebagoes, with remnants of other tribes, carried on an intermittent warfare for years, despite the efforts of the Federal Government to define tribal boundaries; and between red men and white men coveting the same lands causes of irritation were never wanting. In 1827 trouble which had been steadily brewing came to the boiling-point. Predatory expeditions in the north were reported; the Winnebagoes were excited by rumors that another war between the United States and Great Britain was imminent; an incident or even an accident was certain to provoke hostilities. The incident occurred. When Red Bird, a petty Winnebago chieftain dwelling in a "town" on the Black River, was incorrectly informed that two Winnebago braves who had been imprisoned at Prairie du Chien had been executed, he promptly instituted vengeance. A farmer's family in the neighborhood of Prairie du Chien was massacred, and two keel-boats returning down stream from Fort Snelling were attacked, with some loss of life. The settlers hastily repaired the old fort and also dispatched messengers to give the alarm. Galena sent a hundred militiamen; a battalion came down from Fort Snelling; Governor Cass arrived on the spot by way of Green Bay; General Atkinson brought up a full regiment from Jefferson Barracks, near St. Louis; and finally Major Whistler proceeded up the Fox with a portion of the troops stationed at Fort Howard, on Green Bay.

When all was in readiness, the Winnebagoes were notified that, unless Red Bird and his principal accomplice, Wekau, were promptly surrendered, the tribe would be exterminated. The threat had its intended effect, and the two culprits duly presented themselves at Whistler's camp on the Fox-Wisconsin portage, in full savage regalia, and singing their war dirges. Red Bird, who was an Indian of magnificent physique and lofty bearing, had but one request to make - that he be not committed to irons - and this request was granted. At Prairie du Chien, whither the two were sent for trial, he had opportunities to escape, but he refused to violate his word by taking advantage of them. Following their trial, the redskins were condemned to be hanged. Unused to captivity, however, Red Bird languished and soon died, while his accomplice was pardoned by President Adams. In 1828 Fort Winnebago was erected on the site of Red Bird's surrender.

The Winnebagoes now agreed to renounce forever their claims to the lead mines. Furthermore, in the same year, the site of the principal Sauk village and burying-ground, on Rock River, three miles south of the present city of Rock Island, was sold by the Government, and the Sauk and Foxes resident in the vicinity were given notice to leave. Under the Sauk chieftain Keokuk most of the dispossessed warriors withdrew peacefully beyond the Mississippi, and two years later the tribal representatives formally yielded all claims to lands east of that stream. Some members of the tribe, however, established themselves on the high bluff which has since been known as Black Hawk's Watch Tower and defied the Government to remove them.

The leading spirit in this protest was Black Hawk, who though neither born a chief nor elected to that dignity, had long been influential in the village and among his people at large. During the War of 1812 he became an implacable enemy of the Americans, and, after fighting with the British at the battles of Frenchtown and the Thames, he returned to Illinois and carried on a border warfare which ended only with the signing of a special treaty of peace in 1816. For years thereafter he was accustomed to lead his "British band" periodically across northern Illinois and southern Michigan to the British Indian agency to receive presents of arms, ammunition, provisions, and trinkets; and he was a principal intermediary in the British intrigues which gave Cass, as superintendent of Indian affairs in the Northwest, many uneasy days. He was ever a restless spirit and a promoter of trouble, although one must admit that he had some justice on his side and that he was probably honest and sincere. Tall, spare, with pinched features, exceptionally high cheekbones, and a prominent Roman nose, he was a figure to command attention - the more so by reason of the fact that he had practically no eyebrows and no hair except a scalp-lock, in which on state occasions he fastened a flaming bunch of dyed eagle feathers.

Returning from their hunt in the spring of 1830, Black Hawk and his warriors found the site of their town preempted by white settlers and their ancestral burying-ground ploughed over. In deep rage, they set off for Malden, where they were liberally entertained and encouraged to rebel. Coming again to the site of their village a year later, they were peremptorily ordered away. This time they resolved to stand their ground, and Black Hawk ordered the squatters themselves to withdraw and gave them until the middle of the next day to do so. Black Hawk subsequently maintained that he did not mean to threaten bloodshed. But the settlers so construed his command and deluged Governor Reynolds with petitions for help. With all possible speed, sixteen hundred volunteers and ten companies of United States regulars were dispatched to the scene, and on the 25th of June, they made an impressive demonstration within view of the village. In the face of such odds discretion seemed the better part of valor, and during the succeeding night Black Hawk and his followers quietly paddled across the Mississippi. Four days later they signed an agreement never to return to the eastern banks without express permission from the United States Government.

On the Indian side this compact was not meant to be kept. Against the urgent advice of Keokuk and other leaders, Black Hawk immediately began preparations for a campaign of vengeance. British intrigue lent stimulus, and a crafty "prophet," who was chief of a village some thirty-five miles up the Rock, made it appear that aid would be given by the Potawatomi, Winnebagoes, and perhaps other powerful peoples. In the first week of April, 1832, the disgruntled leader and about five hundred braves, with their wives and children, crossed the Mississippi at Yellow Banks and ascended the Rock River to the prophet's town, with a view to raising a crop of corn during the summer and taking the war-path in the fall.

The invasion created much alarm throughout the frontier country. The settlers drew together about the larger villages, which were put as rapidly as possible in a state of defense. Again the Governor called for volunteers, and again the response more than met the expectation. Four regiments were organized, and to them were joined four hundred regulars. One of the first persons to come forward with an offer of his services was a tall, ungainly, but powerful young man from Sangamon County, who had but two years before settled in the State, and who was at once honored with the captaincy of his company. This man was Abraham Lincoln. Other men whose names loom large in American history were with the little army also. The commander of the regulars was Colonel Zachary Taylor. Among his lieutenants were Jefferson Davis and Albert Sidney Johnston, and Robert Anderson, the defender of Fort Sumter in 1860, was a colonel of Illinois volunteers. It is said that the oath of allegiance was administered to young Lincoln by Lieutenant Jefferson Davis!

Over marshy trails and across streams swollen by the spring thaws the army advanced to Dixon's Ferry, ninety miles up the Rock, whence a detachment of three hundred men was sent out, under Major Stillman, to reconnoitre. Unluckily, this force seized three messengers of peace dispatched by Black Hawk and, in the clash which followed, was cut to pieces and driven into headlong flight by a mere handful of red warriors. The effect of this unexpected affray was both to stiffen the Indians to further resistance and to precipitate a fresh panic throughout the frontier. All sorts of atrocities ensued, and Black Hawk's name became a household bugaboo the country over.

Finally a new levy was made ready and sent north. Pushing across the overflowed wilderness stretches, past the sites of modern Beloit and Madison, this army, four thousand strong, came upon the fleeing enemy on the banks of the Wisconsin River, and at Wisconsin Heights, near the present town of Prairie du Sac, it inflicted a severe defeat upon the Indians. Again Black Hawk desired to make peace, but again he was frustrated, this time by the lack of an interpreter. The redskins' flight was continued in the direction of the Mississippi, which they reached in midsummer. They were prevented from crossing by lack of canoes, and finally the half-starved band found itself caught between the fire of a force of regulars on the land side and a government supply steamer, the Warrior, on the water side, and between these two the Indian band was practically annihilated.

Thus ended the war - a contest originating in no

general uprising or far-reaching plan, such as marked the rebellions instigated by Pontiac and Tecumseh, but which none the less taxed the strength of the border populations and opened a new chapter in the history of the remoter northwestern territories. Black Hawk himself took refuge with the Winnebagoes in the Dells of the Wisconsin, only to be treacherously delivered over to General Street at Prairie du Chien. Under the terms of a treaty of peace signed at Fort Armstrong (Rock Island) in September, the fallen leader and some of his accomplices were held as hostages, and during the ensuing winter they were kept at Jefferson Barracks (St. Louis) under the surveillance of Jefferson Davis. In the spring of 1833 they were taken to Washington, where they had an interview with President Jackson. "We did not expect to conquer the whites," Black Hawk told the President; "they had too many houses, too many men. I took up the hatchet, for my part, to revenge injuries which my people could no longer endure. Had I borne them longer without striking, my people would have said, 'Black Hawk is a woman - he is too old to be a chief he is no Sauk.'" After a brief imprisonment at Fortress Monroe, where Jefferson Davis was himself confined at the close of the Civil War, the captives were set free, and were taken to Philadelphia, New York, up the Hudson, and finally back to the Rock River country.

For some years Black Hawk lived quietly on a small reservation near Des Moines. In 1837 the peace-loving Keokuk took him with a party of Sauk and Fox chiefs again to Washington, and on this trip he made a visit to Boston. The officials of the city received the august warrior and his companions in Faneuil Hall, and the Governor of the commonwealth paid them similar honor at the State House. Some war-dances were performed on the Common for the amusement of the populace, and afterwards the party was taken to see a performance by Edwin Forrest at the Tremont Theatre. Here all went well, except that at an exciting point in the play where one of the characters fell dying the Indians burst out into a war-whoop, to the considerable consternation of the women and children present.

A few months after returning to his Iowa home, Black Hawk, now seventy-one years of age, was gathered to his fathers. He was buried about half a mile from his cabin, in a sitting posture, his left hand grasping a cane presented to him by Henry Clay, and at his side a supply of food and tobacco sufficient to last him to the spirit land, supposed to be three days' travel. "Rock River," he said in a speech at a Fourth of July celebration shortly before his death, "was a beautiful country. I liked my town, my cornfields, and the home of my people. I fought for it. It is now yours. Keep it, as we did. It will produce you good crops."

The Black Hawk War opened a new chapter in the history of the Northwest. The soldiers carried to their homes remarkable stories of the richness and attractiveness of the northern country, and the eastern newspapers printed not only detailed accounts of the several expeditions but highly colored descriptions of the charms of the region. Books and pamphlets by the score helped to attract the attention of the country. The result was a heavy influx of settlers, many of them coming all the way from New England and New York, others from Pennsylvania and Ohio. Lands were rapidly surveyed and placed on sale, and surviving Indian hunting-grounds were purchased. Northern Illinois filled rapidly with a thrifty farming population, and the town of Chicago became an entrepot. Further north, Wisconsin had been organized, in 1836, as a Territory, including not only the present State of that name but Iowa, Minnesota, and most of North and South Dakota. As yet the Iowa country, however, had been visited by few white people; and such as came were only hunters and trappers, agents of the American Fur and other trading companies, or independent traders. Two of the most active of these free-lances of early days - the French Canadian Dubuque and the Englishman Davenport - have left their names to flourishing cities.

To recount the successive purchases by which the Government freed Iowa soil from Indian domination would be wearisome. The Treaty of 1842 with the Sauks and Foxes is typical. After a sojourn of hardly more than a decade in the Iowa country, these luckless folk were now persuaded to yield all their lands to the United States and retire to a reservation in Kansas. The negotiations were carried out with all due regard for Indian susceptibilities. Governor Chambers, resplendent in the uniform of a brigadier-general of the United States army, repaired with his aides to the appointed rendezvous, and there the chiefs presented themselves, arrayed in new blankets and white deerskin leggings, with full paraphernalia of paint, feathers, beads, and elaborately decorated war clubs. Oratory ran freely, although through the enforced medium of an interpreter. The chiefs harangued for hours not only upon the beautiful meadows, the running streams, the stately trees, and the other beloved objects which they were called upon to surrender to the white man, but upon the moon and stars and rain and hail and wind, all of which were alleged to be more attractive and beneficent in Iowa than anywhere else. The Governor, in turn, gave the Indians some good advice, urging them to live peaceably in their new homes, to be industrious and self-supporting, to leave liquor alone, and, in general, to "be a credit to the country." When every one had talked as much as he liked, the treaty was solemnly signed.

The "New Purchase" was thrown open to settlers in the following spring; and the opening brought scenes of a kind destined to be reenacted scores of times in the great West during succeeding decades - the borders of the new district lined, on the eve of the opening, with encamped settlers and their families ready to race for the best claims; horses saddled and runners picked for the rush; a midnight signal from the soldiery, releasing a flood of eager land-hunters armed with torches, axes, stakes, and every sort of implement for the laying out of claims with all possible speed; by daybreak, many scores of families "squatting" on the best pieces of ground which they had been able to reach; innumerable disputes, with a general readjustment following the intervention of the government surveyors.

The marvelous progress of the upper Mississippi Valley is briefly told by a succession of dates. In 1838 Iowa was organized as a Territory; in 1846 it was admitted as a State; in 1848 Wisconsin was granted statehood; and in 1849 Minnesota was given territorial organization with boundaries extending westward to the Missouri.

Thus the Old Northwest had arrived at the goal set for it by the large-visioned men who framed the Ordinance of 1787; every foot of its soil was included in some one of the five thriving, democratic commonwealths that had taken their places in the Union on a common basis with the older States of the East and the South. Furthermore, the Mississippi had ceased to be a boundary. A magnificent vista reaching off to the remoter West and Northwest had been opened up; the frontier had been pushed far out upon the plains of Minnesota and Iowa. Decade after decade the powerful epic of westward expansion, shot through with countless tales of heroism and sacrifice, had steadily unfolded before the gaze of an astonished world; and the end was not yet in sight.

Bibliographical Note

There is no general history of the Northwest covering the whole of the period dealt with in this book except Burke A. Hinsdale, The Old Northwest (1888). This is a volume of substantial scholarship, though it reflects but faintly the life and spirit of the people. The nearest approach to a moving narrative is James K. Hosmer, "Short History of the Mississippi Valley" (1901), which tells the story of the Middle West from the earliest explorations to the close of the nineteenth century, within a brief space, yet in a manner to arouse the reader's interest and sympathy. A fuller and very readable narrative to 1796 will be found in Charles Moore, "The Northwest under Three Flags" (1900). Still more detailed, and enlivened by many contemporary rasps and plans, is Justin Winsor, "The Westward Movement" (1899), covering the period from the pacification of 1763 to the close of the eighteenth century. Frederick J. Turner, "Rise of the New West" (1906) contains several interesting and authoritative chapters on western development after the War of 1812; and John B. McMaster, "History of the People of the United States" (8 vols., 1883-1913), gives in the fourth and fifth volumes a very good account of westward migration.

An excellent detailed account of the settlement and development of a single section of the Northwest is G.

N. Fuller, "Economic and Social Beginnings of Michigan," Michigan Historical Publications, Univ. Series, No.1 (1916). A very readable book is R. G. Thwaites, "The Story of Wisconsin" (rev. ed., 1899), containing a full account of the early relations of white men and red men, and of the Black Hawk War. Mention may be made, too, of H. E. Legler, "Leading Events of Wisconsin History" (1898).

Among the volumes dealing with the diplomatic history of the Northwest, mention should be made of two recent studies: C. W. Alvord, "The Mississippi Valley in British Politics" (2 vols., 1917), and E. S. Corwin, "French Policy and the American Alliance" (1916).

Aside from Lincoln, few men of the earlier Northwest have been made the subjects of well-written biographies. Curiously, there are no modern biographies, good or bad, of George Rogers Clark, General St. Clair, or William Henry Harrison. John R. Spears, "Anthony Wayne" (1903) is an interesting book; and Andrew C. McLaughlin, "Lewis Cass" (1891), and Allen Johnson, "Stephen A. Douglas" (1908) are excellent. Lives of Lincoln that have importance for their portrayal of western society include: John T. Morse, Jr., "Abraham Lincoln" (2 vols., 1893); John G. Nicolay and John Hay, "Abraham Lincoln, a History" (10 vols., 1890); and Ida M. Tarbell, "Life of Abraham Lincoln" (new ed., 2vols., 1917).

The reader will do well, however, to turn early to some of the works within the field which, by reason of their literary quality as well as their scholarly worth, have attained the dignity of classics. Foremost are the writings of Francis Parkman. Most of these, it is true, deal with the history of the American interior prior to 1763. But "Frontenac and New France under Louis XIV" (Frontenac edition, 1915), and "A Half-Century of Conflict" (2 vols., same ed.) furnish the necessary background; and "The Conspiracy of Pontiac" (2 vols., same ed.) is indispensable. Parkman's work closes with the Indian war following the Treaty of 1763. Theodore Roosevelt's "Winning of the West" (4 vols., 1889-96) takes up the story at that point and carries it to the collapse of the Burr intrigues during the second administration of Thomas Jefferson. This work was a pioneer in the field. In the light of recent scholarship it is subject to criticism at some points; but it is based on careful study of the sources, and for vividness and interest it has perhaps not been surpassed in American historical writing. A third extensive work is Archer B. Hulbert, "Historic Highways of America" (16 vols., 1902-05). In writing the history of the great land and water routes of trade and travel between East and West the author found occasion to describe, in interesting fashion, most phases of western life. The volumes most closely related to the subject matter of the present book are: "Military Roads of the Mississippi Valley" (VIII); "Waterways of Western Expansion" (IX); "The Cumberland Road" (X); and "Pioneer Roads and Experiences of Travellers" (XIXII). Mention should be made also of Mr. Hulbert's "The Ohio River, a Course of Empire" (1906).

Further references will be found appended to the articles on Illinois, Indiana, Michigan, Ohio, and Wisconsin in "The Encyclopaedia Britannica" (11th edition).

Opportunity to get the flavor of the period by reading

contemporary literature is afforded by two principal kinds of books. One is reminiscences, letters, and histories written by the Westerners themselves. Timothy Flint's "Recollections of the Last Ten Years" (1826) will be found interesting; as also J. Hall, "Letters from the West" (1828), and T. Ford, "History of Illinois" (1854).

The second type of materials is books of travel written by visitors from the East or from Europe. Works of this nature are always subject to limitations. Even when the author tries to be accurate and fair, his information is likely to be hastily gathered and incomplete and his judgments unsound. Between 1800 and 1840 the Northwest was visited, however, by many educated and fair-minded persons who wrote readable and trustworthy descriptions of what they saw and heard. A complete list cannot be given here, but some of the best of these books are: John Melish, "Travels in the United States of America in the Years 1806 & 1807 and 1809, 1810 & 1811" (2 vols., 1810; William Cobbett, A Year's Residence in the United States of America (1818); Henry B. Fearon, Sketches of America (1818); Morris Birkbeck, Letters from Illinois (1818); John Bradbury, Travels in the Interior of America in the Years 1809, 1810, and 1811" (1819); Thomas Hulme, "Journal made during a Tour in the Western Countries of America, 1818-1819" (1828); and Michael Chevalier, "Society, Manners, and Politics in the United States" (1839). Copies of early editions of some of these works will be found in most large libraries. But the reader is happily not dependent on this resource. Almost all of the really important books of the kind are reprinted, with introductions and explanatory matter, in Reuben G. Thwaites, "Early Western Travels, 1714-1846" (32 vols., 1904-07), which is one of our chief collections of historical materials.

www.ingramcontent.com/pod-product-compliance
Lightning Source LLC
Chambersburg PA
CBHW020002050426
42450CB00005B/284